THE LITERARY FALLACY

THE PATTEN FOUNDATION

Mr. Will Patten of Indianapolis (A.B., Indiana University, 1893) made in 1931 a gift for the establishment of the Patten Foundation at his Alma Mater. Under the terms of this gift, which became available upon the death of Mr. Patten (May 3, 1936), there is to be chosen each year a Visiting Professor who is to be in residence several weeks during the year. The purpose of this prescription is to provide an opportunity for members and friends of the University to enjoy the privilege and advantage of personal acquaintance with the Visiting Professor. The Visiting Professor for the Patten Foundation in 1942–1943 was

Mr. Bernard DeVoto

BERNARD DeVOTO

The
Literary Fallacy

KENNIKAT PRESS, INC./PORT WASHINGTON, N. Y.

To

R. CARLYLE BULEY
and
CECIL K. BYRD

We lived to see God break their bitter charms,
God and the good Republic come riding back in
arms:
We have seen the city of Mansoul, even as it
rocked, relieved —
Blessed are they who did not see, but being blind,
believed.

Preface 9721?

THIS book consists of lectures which I delivered on the Patten Foundation at Indiana University in March, 1943. In preparing them for publication I have considerably expanded a preliminary statement which was part of the first lecture and have set it off as Chapter 1. I have also eliminated a number of expressions required by platform delivery, and have supplied footnotes to two chapters which were tolerably close-packed without them.

I am indebted to Wallace Stegner for checking my account of John Wesley Powell, to Dr. Robert Henry Aldrich for helping me through the history of burns, and to Mrs. N. Preston Breed for preparing the typescript and reading the proofs.

BERNARD DeVOTO

Cambridge, Massachusetts
November 1, 1943

Contents

THE LITERARY FALLACY

Say Now Shibboleth

SINCE WAYS of thinking are fairly constant, the fallacy which this book examines is likely to appear in some of the reviews of the book in literary periodicals. Readers who may want to see the fallacy in actual operation are advised to look for it there. The book is not a history of American literature during the 1920's but some reviewers will probably assume that it means to be and others that it ought to be, and both will treat it as if it were. It does not try to describe American literature during the 1920's completely, to tell the whole truth about it, or to pass judgment on it as a whole, but some reviewers may report on it in an understanding that it tries to do all three. It does not try to analyze any writer or any book completely, or to pass final judgment on any, but some reviewers are likely to conclude that it tries to do what I point out it does not, and they will discuss it as a projection of their own sentiments. In order to prevent its being thought of as a history of the period's literature, a comprehensive description, or an analysis in absolute terms, I have burdened the text with reservations and qualifications up to the limit of the reader's patience, or beyond it. Some reviewers may not be aware of those reservations and others may ignore them. Such reviewers will be acting in good faith, with no awareness of misunderstanding the book and no intention of misrepresenting it. But also they will be acting from preconceptions or according to imperatives which frequently characterize the way of thinking herein examined.

Well, what is this book? It is an examination, reasonably detailed but far from complete, of certain ideas, dogmas, and conclusions which appear and reappear in much American literature of the 1920's, particularly in the work of writers who were then widely held to be most characteristic of the time and most expressive of its spirit. Whatever their context, they are literary ideas, dogmas, and conclusions. Sometimes they appear in considerable purity and intensity, as principal or even exclusive themes. Sometimes they are mixed, weak, or tangential. Sometimes they appear as assumptions or prepossessions rather than theses, or as reflections of the theses of others, or as tones or overtones of belief rather than formulated opinions. Sometimes they color a writer's work only a little. Sometimes they appear in the books of the same writer, or even in the same book, with varying degrees of intensity. My purpose is to examine various appearances of these ideas, dogmas, and conclusions, to appraise their validity, and to study some of the relationships among them.

I try, that is, to isolate for examination a phenomenon which I have called the literary fallacy, though it is not a formal fallacy but rather a complex of fallacies in logic, defects in observation and understanding, and errors in fact. This effort sometimes requires me to partly separate the fallacy from its context. Sometimes it requires me to disregard the qualities of a book which commend it to readers. I am aware of those facts, have frequently called attention to them, and ask the reader to bear in mind that I am not making esthetic judgments. My description of the literary fallacy is not complete. It is a first approximation, a triangulation rather than a map. It finally centers on two principal sentiments, weightier than the sum of all the rest, which underlie the ideas, dogmas, and judgments examined here. In the literature which this book examines they frequently coincide and they are never altogether separated. They, their relationships, and the subsidiary ideas, dogmas, and judgments which stem from them are, according to my findings, characteristic of a way of thinking. I study that way of thinking as it found literary expression during the 1920's, but it did not originate in that decade and it has not ceased to operate.

Do my findings say more than that some writers were ignorant, some in error, some inaccurate, some frivolous, some foolish, and some corrupt? If that were all, still there would be relevance in saying it at this time. Once more there is going on a widespread effort to examine the American people, describe their past, and assess their culture. There is point in reminding the unliterary person, the general reader, that during the 1920's leading writers did not usually try to control or correct one another's ignorance, inaccuracy, or folly, that they did not conceive themselves or one another to be ignorant, inaccurate, or foolish, and that it remains possible still for writers to be ignorant, inaccurate, foolish, or all three.

But there is a more important point. It was not from desire and prime intent that the writers herein discussed were ignorant, inaccurate, or foolish — or frivolous or corrupt. Quite the contrary. Usually they understood themselves to be dedicated, by intentions altogether idealistic, to a truth-telling which they understood to be rigorous and onerous. What betrayed them was not folly or frivolity of purpose but a way of thinking — an intricate system of propositions, assumptions, predispositions, and axioms, plus a method of logically manipulating them toward conclusions. That way of thinking is my chief interest here.

That way of thinking is not exclusively a possession of literary people. Literary people, in fact, are its least important proprietors, and the serious damage it has done in our time lies outside literature. But this book — a series of lectures to college students — is confined to its application inside literature. I have chosen an era earlier than the 1920's to study, as a historian, the effect in social actions of *a priori* reasoning, monism, absolutism, uncontrolled generalization, and the nested errors of subjective description. The rich field of the 1920's I leave to other students. It is almost untouched, the research will be fascinating, and trustworthy studies are not only desirable, they are absolutely necessary for immediate use. But I also cherish a private hope that veterans of the 1920's, some of whom remain to us in full vigor, may take up such a study in the light of new principles which they have acquired while following new plows. An examination from new premises of social actions in the United States during the 1920's by one who, during the 1920's, applied to those actions the way of thinking discussed here would be at least invigorating. Comedy, one of them remarked in a different connection, has obligations which it dare not evade.

A British broadcaster, speaking to the people of nations conquered by the Nazis, employed a striking symbol, the opening four notes of Beethoven's Fifth Symphony, which in International Morse give *V*. To people who lived in darkness it meant hope, victory, liberation, restoration: many of them died for it. But presently newsreels were showing us baseball players making the *V*-for-Victory sign while they raised a championship pennant over the home park, candidates for the common council with upraised fingers on election day, and the press agents of movie actresses gesturing the same dauntlessness at popularity contests. Soon Fifth Avenue took it up and you could see *V*'s in Roman or International on women's veils, handkerchiefs, scarves, and handbags, where they gave chic and salesmanship a mutually gratifying expression. *Harper's Bazaar* having taken a profit from the hopes and deaths of enslaved people, the fashion spread to Fifty-second Street, which engraved the symbol on cocktail glasses, and to Broadway, which set it in rhinestones over the navels of chorus girls. Whatever it meant to men and women in the Warsaw ghetto who risked death to listen for it at midnight, it signified nothing much in New York night clubs.

British aviators going out to bomb the Continent added the gremlin to the company of fabulous creatures who in all ages have helped men to explain the unknown and to mock death. Gremlins were a meaningful fancy to men risking their lives in the course of duty; humor and resolution were in their birth. But within a few weeks picture magazines, comic strips, and radio programs made them a vulgar and offensive fad.

Similarly silly fads are always with us in the catch-phrases which seem to arise as by-products of the vigorous functioning of the American language. Lately we have seen two such fashions. The dislocation of the conjunction "but" carries a suggestion of Park Avenue. If at proper times and in proper contexts you say "But beautiful" or "I'm dead, but exhausted," the usage shows that you are an initiate, that you are at ease with the well-heeled, that worldliness and *savoir-faire* are your birth-

right or at any rate an acquired skill. A similar dislocation of the adverb "strictly" also stamps you as an initiate
and insider, but on a lowlier plane. "But" makes you, so
to speak, a Marquand character, whereas "strictly" identifies you as an invention of John O'Hara or Damon
Runyon. Such mannerisms are always bubbling through
ordinary speech. In their early appearances they are
frequently humorous, fresh, or picturesque but they
soon become clichés which offend the fastidious. Some
people use them thoughtlessly, meaninglessly, or auto-
matically. Others, however, use them in a belief that they
are smart and modish, or that they are an expression of
taste or viewpoint, or even that they are profound. They
spread to the radio and the movies. Popular literature,
which has a fast getaway and a short cycle, takes them
up. They begin to appear seriously in the work of serious
writers. Frequently, on their way up they retain their
automatic quality, their meaninglessness, or their illusion
of profundity.

But do I mean that the literary ideas of the 1920's
which I examine here were mere fads, on the level of the
cocktail-bar *V*, the comic-strip gremlin, or the smart
solecism? Do I imply that literary ideas are usually on
that level or perhaps that it does not matter much what
ideas a writer holds? I expect to be held to such questions, on penalty of being shown either to have fouled
my own nest or to have committed a public idiocy. Such
questions, however, cannot be answered. It depends on

what you are talking about and how you are talking about it. It depends on how you think about literature. It depends on how literature thinks about itself.

There are many ways of thinking about literature. There are many ways of thinking about it apart from professional ways, the ways used by writers. Thus, one may think of literature as one of the graces and ornaments of life, a knowledge of which is rewarding to well-rounded and discriminating persons, who will take pleasure in it as they do in the ability to understand the structure of symphonies, to ski skillfully, or to express a sophisticated taste in dress or decoration. That is a dilettante and superficial way of thinking, one which writers do not find congenial. Nevertheless people who think in that way retain a pleasure in reading that is uncommon among writers, and escape the disenchantment with literature which literature has been recording throughout our time. Few people except writers and amateur writers have ever believed that literature is the most important activity of man, and another way of thinking about it is a way common among mature and cultivated practitioners of other disciplines. One might plausibly argue, in fact, that such persons are the ideal audience of writers — who properly do not write for one another or for critics. Their judgment is grounded in wide knowledge and weathered by experience of mankind and the world, they know the labors and skill of craftsmanship, and yet with whatever delight they may approach literature, they can approach it without the imperatives, the compulsive and protective thinking, of writers.

I think of one such man, a physiologist who is now dead. Educated in America, he also studied science in France and Germany and later taught it in France and England. He experienced European cultures deeply and he had the self-reliant pride in his own national and sectional culture without which genuine cosmopolitanism cannot exist. He knew at least four national literatures intimately but literature was an interest of his leisure only, as it must be for all who are not writers. He read literature all his life — eagerly, discriminatingly, sympathetically, and with enjoyment. I stress the last fact, that he read with enjoyment, for his eagerness was seldom disappointed. He never felt the revulsion from literature that writers of our time have repeatedly expressed, and in the twenty years of our friendship I never knew him to make the accusation, which writers of our time have repeatedly made, that literature was failing or had failed. I have never known anyone to whose life literature contributed more.

I cannot make a long parenthesis to analyze what I take to have been this man's — wholly unformulated — principles of literary judgment. He trusted writers to report their own emotions, their experience as they understood it, their perceptions and beliefs and judgments, and to reveal unconsciously much about themselves which they did not report. It was the ability of writers to be articulate about matters which other men could not adequately express. He saw writers as related to their times, as repeating the basic experiences which all men share, and as expressing individual variations of common experience. It never occurred to him that what we call literary experience was of a higher or finer order than his own, or that literary people were final arbiters or interpreters of any experience. In all literature there were exceedingly few writers whom he would have accepted as authorities on anything except the content of their own emotions, and he would not have submitted to poets or dramatists or novelists on the one hand, or to literary critics on the other, questions of final value in morals, politics, or economics. He would read, say, Sinclair Lewis or Ernest Hemingway with great interest, but he had no expectation that they could tell him the meaning of American culture or the meaning of human life. He would read with interest the work of literary thinkers — we must partly distinguish between them and literary artists — but the critic he most admired was Sainte-Beuve and such critics as, say, Lewis Mumford and Allen Tate interested him exclusively as literature. He did not project literary ideas beyond literature, he did not think they could be extended validly, and it was impossible for him to apply literary criteria to life. Van Wyck Brooks's ideas about America, for instance, interested him only as literary ideas — he could grant such writers no greater authority to speak about American society than they had to speak about his own specialty, which happened to be the chemistry of the blood. A literary critic might have interesting ideas about the United States, and he might have interesting ideas about the stability of oxygen in the blood, but his calling gave him no more intrinsic authority over the one than over the other. In fact, the circumstances in which his calling had to be practised suggested beforehand that he was necessarily uninformed about both.

This way of thinking has obvious limitations, it is rather tory than whig, and it is tinged with what is sometimes called Philistinism. It is abhorrent to most writers. I, for instance, am too subdued to what I work in to think of literature in that way. As my argument unfolds you will see that I think of it from radically different bases, with assumptions that exclude or contradict my friend's. But I point out that both of the ways of thinking about literature thus briefly noted, the dilettante's and the discriminating layman's, produce favorable judgments about American literature of the 1920's, as many professional ways of thinking about literature, including mine, do not.

If you do not require of literature the absolute truths and final judgments which literary people usually require of it, or pretend to require, then the literature with which we are concerned is one of the great periods of American literature, and probably the most colorful, vigorous, and exciting period. In the books of literary thinkers America has come of age so frequently that, even forgetting the earlier great ages, it would be tiresome to say that it achieved literary maturity during the

1920's. Yet in at least two ways our literature did come of age then: for the first time it exercised *as a whole* a direct influence on foreign literatures, and its average level of professional competence was higher than that of any preceding period in America. Whereas before the First World War only the isolated great man, an Emerson or Whitman, a Mark Twain or Henry James, had spoken to the world at large, following the war, the themes and techniques, even the fads and follies, of the American literary generation exercised a powerful influence on the work of foreign writers. If no American novelist had the stature of Proust or the virtuosity of Joyce, postwar American fiction as a whole was fresher, more vigorous, and more expert than either French or English fiction as a whole. Two Americans, Pound and Eliot, between them created nearly all the principal poetic modes not only of America but of England as well. Though the Nobel Prize had sometimes fallen to writers as unimportant as Sienkiewicz, Maeterlinck, and Tagore, the climate of literary opinion before the war precluded such a recognition of American literature as an award to an American writer would have implied. In 1907 Oxford University conferred honorary degrees on both Kipling and Mark Twain, but the Nobel Prize, as a matter of course, as a reflex of European valuation of their respective literatures, went to the inferior writer. But when postwar American literature matured, two Nobel Prizes went to Americans equally as a matter of course. The award to Mr. O'Neill was grotesque and the motivation of the award to Mr. Lewis had certain overtones, perhaps, but they signalized a change in European valuations. In the awareness of Europe American literature had ceased to be a tributary of the English current; it had become an integral and sometimes dominant part of world literature of its own right.

Furthermore, in the 1920's there were more competent writers in America than there had ever been before. If there were fewer first-raters than in either of the two principal earlier periods, if no one had the stature of Emerson or Thoreau or Mark Twain, nevertheless the generality of writers were more expert and of higher quality than the generality of writers before them. I have no space to discuss these "good competent workmen, literary people doing a satisfactory job, giving the time back something of its tone and color, amusing it, holding up a more or less accurately surfaced mirror for it to gaze into." In the average they were the liveliest, the most vigorous, the most entertaining writers the United States has ever had. No one who lived and read his way through the Twenties will forget the verve, the excitement of that literature, the sheer animal spirits with which it treated even its most lugubrious themes. Readers will be returning to it for a long time to recapture precisely that excitement, especially readers who do not ask literature to be absolute.

Finally, the literature of the Twenties achieved something like a charter of liberties for American writers. The labors, agonies, and failures of many forgotten writers made the way easier, but of its own will and effort it established the freedom of American writers to write about such subjects as interested them in such ways and from such points of view as seemed best to them — and to do so without odium, interference, or coercion. . . . We must remember that the achievement is not necessarily permanent. In the earliest years of the following decade, in fact, a ferment among the absolutes of literary thinking induced many writers to make a violent assault on the freedom that had been so lately won for them. It will be sagacious to remember that this attempt to enforce a test oath on writers, this effort to impose on literature stated imperatives and a fixed orthodoxy, was made not by American society but by American writers. And if some of those who made it were acting as the stooges of a realistic, foreign, political absolutism, it will be sagacious to remember that also — as a literary rather than a social fact.

From many points of view, then, the literature of the Twenties is a brilliant, various, and rich literature. There remain other ways of looking at it. One way is to think of literature as a fundamental expression of the human spirit, one of the activities of man which dignify his estate, illuminate his experience, work toward truth, pass judgment on life, and try to plumb the mysteries of fate. Writers have usually thought of it in that way, never more unanimously than during the Twenties. That way of thinking about literature is the one adopted in the lectures that follow. I apply to the literature of the

Twenties the standards of value which it told us it had chosen for itself.

〜〜〜

I begin with two of many confessions of failure which in the last three or four years have become characteristic of American literature. Some of them are more nearly accusations than confessions and on the basis of them it would be possible to assert that during the Twenties, in fact during the entire period between the two wars, there had not been, properly speaking, an American literature. They amount to a finding that there has been no literature which was organically a part of American life, but instead an anarchic welter without coherence of its own and without living relationship to its society. In regard to the literature accepted by leading writers themselves as foremost in influence, the literature which I herein call official, that finding is true.

If the accusation has become commonplace, so has one explanation. The defense says that the literature of the Twenties was confused and anarchic because it was faithfully reflecting its times. The failure of literature was a sickness of society. Writers had inherited confusion, anarchy, and despair; such things were their proper themes; out of them they wrote their books. Perhaps future historians will be able to use this literature as symptomatic of the fissures, discordances, and deterioration in American society during the Twenties. I do not think that it will have even that usefulness, but if it does we must bear in mind the distinction between a description and a case history. That Mr. Hemingway wrote *The Sun Also Rises* does not necessarily diagnose the sickness from which you and I may be suffering, it does not even establish the fact that we are not feeling well. The truth is that literature's repudiation of American life during the Twenties shut it away from the realities of that life, the evils as well as the good. The verdict of those future historians is likely to be that the evils of American society are not portrayed or even reflected in the literature which, some historians may say, should have accepted the obligation to explore them.

But what is the point of remembering merely literary folly during wartime? Why should I, invited by the Trustees of Indiana University to address young men and women who will presently be taking an active part in the war, spend my time and theirs discussing a literature which I hold to have misrepresented its time and which, it is already clear, I believe to be of no great value?

Well, another development of the last few years, as a realization of our catastrophe has come upon us, has been a widespread resolution to examine the mistakes which we now know we have made, in the hope of avoiding similar ones hereafter. A generation which must fight a war to turn the world back toward rationality would be lost indeed if war were its only means of repairing mistakes. Literature has been telling you that the generation of your fathers — my generation — made the mistakes for which your generation has to pay with its lives or at best with the sacrifice of its expectations. Literature has told you, in fact, rather more about those mistakes than is true. But if the mistakes of my generation are responsible for your disaster, then we must do what we can to explain how they happened. The literature of my generation has made mistakes. They have affected you and they are part of the confusion that has engulfed you. Literature has given you some ideas which are erroneous and built into your thinking misrepresentations and fallacies which impair the instruments you must use. Clearness of mind requires these errors, fallacies, and misrepresentations to be described. A generation which confesses — with perhaps a little less or a little more than the truth — that it has failed owes its heirs an analysis of failure. A literary generation which tells you that it has misguided you owes you an explanation of how and wherein, though usually from altogether admirable motives, it fell into error. The subject of these lectures is some of the mistakes of American literature in our time — not all of them for I am not an encyclopedist of folly. I hope to explain to you one way in which our literature has betrayed its trust — or, if that phrase is pretentious, one way in which literature has been less than it has pretended to be.

There may be a further justification for discussing this particular subject at this particular time. Presently I shall be showing that the general effort of American literature during the 1920's was to write a description of the United States, its people, its history, and its culture — and that the one uniformity in it is the agreement of writers to the description achieved. There happens to be another description of the United States, its people, its history, and its culture, written by other hands. A representative part of it may be examined in, for example, the works of Oswald Spengler (especially those later than *The Decline of the West*) and a long series of treatises which issued from Professor Haushofer's institute of geopolitics. That description of the United States as a decadent pluto-democracy, and its people as degenerate, forms the basis of Adolf Hitler's understanding of America in *Mein Kampf* and elsewhere, and of countless millions of words broadcast for many years by the propaganda agencies of Nazi Germany. Unquestionably the masters of the *Reich* accepted that description of America as accurate — they based on it a large part of their calculations for the war that was to give them mastery of the world. But there is a striking correspondence between the Spenglerian and geopolitical description of America on the one hand and, on the other, the description of America embodied in American literature of the 1920's. The correspondence is so obvious, so often an identity, that there must be a causal relationship between them. Clearly the master race accepted in good faith the description of America which American writers had provided, and made their plans in accordance with it. I am not obliged to determine whether a decade of our literature thus invited our enemies to aggressions which they might not otherwise have dared or hoaxed them to their doom. But it seems desirable to point out another way in which casual literary idealisms may store up debts that call for payments wholly unforeseen by literary men.

II

Oh, Lost America!

LET US ask a question, briefly answer it, and set the answer aside as a bench mark to return to later. Select a number of writers who any informed critic will agree were leading and characteristic writers of the period. Select, say, H. L. Mencken, Sinclair Lewis, Ernest Hemingway, John Dos Passos, William Falkner, and Thomas Wolfe. If someone who was ignorant of American life during the 1920's were to consult the books of these men in an effort to understand it, could he use their work as a trustworthy guide? Does the picture which their work contains correspond to American experience and could our stranger rely on it when he came to appraise our culture? Is it trustworthy data for historians who may hope to inform future generations about our past?

The answer is no. Add an observation to it. You, who lack firsthand experience of American life during part of the time covered by the work of those writers, have in part used their work as a basis for your judgments of that

time. And already historians have appeared who, undertaking to pass judgment on that time for the guidance of
future readers, have confidently accepted the work of
those men as a sufficient and trustworthy representation
of it. There is, to name one, Mr. Maxwell Geismar. Mr.
Geismar has written a book, *Writers in Crisis*, to explain
and appraise a number of writers, among them some of
those I have named. He sees much in them to praise and
something, though not much, to condemn. But nowhere
in his book does he squarely face the possibility that
what they reported about the life they were dealing with
may have been insufficient, inaccurate, or untrue. If, very
rarely, he suspects that one of them has been misled, he
comfortably refers to another one to correct him, and
moves on. In good faith he accepts their description as
he finds it, in good faith he transmits it to those who
may read him, and in good faith he writes a description
of that, to him, long vanished time. So after a conscien-
tiously logical analysis — of books — Mr. Geismar con-
structs an edifice which he believes faithfully contains
the times it deals with but which anyone who has lived
through that time recognizes as almost entirely myth.
The bricks it is built of are the faulty or false reports
of his predecessors. Because he accepts the descriptions
and interpretations of such men as I have named, he goes
atrociously wrong in his understanding of their time.
He asks his readers to accept his understanding. But to
accept it would be to perpetuate misrepresentation and
in the end make it irreparable. As a map of the past his

book is false. Anyone who might use it would be disastrously misled, for the angles of divergence, the errors, even if minute to begin with, would lead him farther astray with every moment of time and every foot of space traveled. Mr. Geismar's book illustrates the process by which one literary generation's errors become the next one's illusions. It is completely inclosed by the literary fallacy.

For several years one of the leading writers of our time, Mr. Archibald MacLeish, has been periodically attacking the writers of our time for having betrayed our culture, freely confessing that, in an earlier period of unenlightenment, he was one of those who betrayed it. I make the same accusation, but if I agree with Mr. MacLeish's finding I cannot agree with his analysis.

In 1940 Mr. MacLeish made a powerful, organized, passionate attack on modern American literature which he called *The Irresponsibles*. It brought a good many writers down from the high place shouting "Fascist!" at Mr. MacLeish. We may disregard the epithet, which is preposterous, intellectually dishonest, and a symptom of the very irresponsibility which Mr. MacLeish denounced. Except in a small number of cases, cases which, furthermore, writers have not usually had the wit to recognize, the epithet "Fascist" applied by writers to one another has meant one or the other of two things. It has meant either "I disagree with him" or "He does not like my books." Now Mr. MacLeish's finding, that on the whole two decades of American literature have been a betrayal of our culture, is, I believe, just. But his analysis of the betrayal is a mirror image of the facts. He says that the irresponsibility of writers in our time consists in their devotion to conveying faithfully and exactly the true nature of things as they are. In other words, objectively reporting what they truly and accurately see. A generalization about American literature in our time could hardly be more completely wrong. It is the exact opposite of the truth. If American writers of our time had objectively reported the nature of American life in our time, it might still be possible to object to them but it would be impossible to make the particular objection which Mr. MacLeish made. The prime error of American literature between wars was its failure to report objectively the nature of American life. The rest of what I have to say to you will be devoted to some of the fallacies that produced the error which Mr. MacLeish misconceives.

Turn now to Mr. Van Wyck Brooks, who in 1941 repeated Mr. MacLeish's accusation, that modern American literature has been in the main a betrayal of American life. He also brought out writers on the run hurling stones and shouting "Fascist!" The epithet was equally irresponsible and dishonest, and if it was shouted more loudly at Mr. Brooks that would appear to be because he mentioned by name more writers whose books he did not like. I quote a part of Mr. Brooks's finding: —

> Is there any one respect in which the literature of our time . . . differs from the literature of previous ages? . . . I think it has one trait, and one that

is striking in a perspective now of twenty-five years; and this is that writers have ceased to be *voices of the people.* . . . Preponderantly, our literature of the last quarter-century has been the expression of self-conscious intellectuals who do not even wish to be voices of the people. Some of these writers have labored *for* the people; they have fought valiant fights for social justice. But their perceptions have not been *of* the people. . . . Some again . . . wish, without surrendering their literary standards, to make themselves voices of the people. . . . This is a way of saying that the literary mind of our time is sick. It has lost its roots in the soil of mankind, although it possesses a certain energy. I think it has great energy, which makes the phenomenon all the more glaring. In other words, our literature is *off-center.* . . . [Contemporary writers] had cut themselves off from mankind and formed a circle of their own that was wholly out of relation to the springs of life. They had broken their organic bonds with family life, the community, nature, and they wrote in a private language of personal friends; they felt nothing but contempt for the primary realities, which they had ceased to feel and completely ignored, and human wisdom played no part in the system of esthetics that characterized their artificial world. They lived with their fixed ideas in a vacuum; they were the victims of inbreeding, poisoning one another with their despair and poisoning society

also; and they had come to represent the suicide of
the human spirit. . . .

That quotation accurately describes the aspects of
contemporary literature which I have chosen to deal
with here, and it is a deeper and more accurate analysis
than Mr. MacLeish's. In both his description and his
analysis, Mr. Brooks covers much more ground than this
quotation. Much of what he says beyond it is true; much
is, I think, wrong. But I remind you of my purpose. I
am trying to anatomize certain aspects only of literature
and to lay open some of the errors that produced them.
It is a limited purpose.

When two so different minds as Mr. MacLeish and
Mr. Brooks report the fact identically, I need not rest
the betrayal of our culture by contemporary literature
on my own assertion. But there are reasons why Mr.
Brooks's finding is an exceedingly striking item in literary
history. For though both Mr. MacLeish and Mr. Brooks
repudiate the literature of their generation, Mr. Brooks
is repudiating a literature which, in some part, he begot.
Literary forces are seldom as effective as critics believe,
but Mr. Brooks was truly an active agent in shaping the
literature of the 1920's. In the area of literary ideas he
was an analyst, expositor, and propagandist more bril-
liantly effective than any of his contemporaries. Some of
the key literary ideas of the time are his creations; others
he developed more resolutely and profoundly than anyone else. Furthermore, he made disciples, who became an

influential coterie. Many writers of less original intelligence took over his ideas whole and began to expand and apply them. The careers of many others consist exclusively of searching out specific illustrations of his general ideas. Much of the structure of ideas which the 1920's built is unmistakably his, and if in time he came to object to many of its wings, ells, and porches, the pat answer of many writers whom he rejected could have been that he made the bricks which they used and which, furthermore, they merely laid down on foundations which he had erected for them. In the words of the grace they might have been content to say, "Of thine own, Lord, do we return unto Thee."

It is therefore proper to begin our examination of literary fallacies by examining some of the ideas of Van Wyck Brooks.

Mr. Brooks's work falls into two parts, the books he wrote before his ideas reversed themselves and those which he wrote afterward.[1] In my next lecture I show how the same way of thinking produced diametrically opposite results, but we are now concerned with his earlier books, particularly *America's Coming-of-Age*, published in 1915, and *Letters and Leadership*, published in 1918. In his later period Mr. Brooks first tacitly recanted the ideas of these books and then explicitly disavowed them. In the meantime, however, they had served as working blueprints for the literature of the 1920's. To a very large extent the postwar literature of America (though we must not forget that it had begun to take shape before the war began) was an effort to describe and appraise the culture of America, past and present.[2] To an equally large extent that effort employed as tools the ideas which Mr. Brooks had forged for it in the books I have named.

We must, however, phrase Mr. Brooks's own effort a little differently: he set out to describe and appraise American society. He took his stand on a thesis which, twenty years later, the proletarian coterie were to denounce him for ignoring: the thesis that the duty of writers is to work directly with society. (But at the same time, and with great confusion, he vigorously insisted that the use of any but purely artistic concepts was a lethal error.) As his part in the belated maturing of American life, as his contribution to the symphony for which (at last) he heard the fiddles tuning all over America, he intended to anatomize our society, chart the course of its development, and pass final judgment on it.

It is of primary importance to observe that Mr. Brooks approached American society first (and, so it was later to prove, exclusively) by way of literature. It is also important to observe that the literature by way of which he brought our society to judgment was that which the college textbooks of the time, Barrett Wendell's for instance, accepted as classic: the famous New Englanders, Poe, Mark Twain, Whitman, and for the modern note Howells and Henry James, who were still living when he began to write. It was a thin choice, a conventional and even reactionary choice, but he made it in good faith. In the first place, the inability to credit the reality of any portion of the country except New England, which extends to his later books, was central in the literary tradition which he accepted. In the second place, as time was to show, he did not know any American literature beyond that which academic criticism had established as orthodox. There is no mention of Melville, for instance, in these early books.[3] There are allusions to N. P. Willis and Bayard Taylor, conventional textbook figures, but no mention of contemporaries who worked in main currents of American literature. There are references to Jack London and a remark which I take to refer to Frank Norris, but otherwise the entire period on whose shoulders Mr. Brooks is standing goes unmentioned. (He appears to have read Theodore Dreiser between these two books. In a book of his adolescence, *The Wine of the Puritans*, there is a young sneer which inquires why he should pay any attention to a poet whom Theodore Roosevelt had praised — Roosevelt was necessarily an uncultural figure since no one had arisen to classify him as an imaginative writer. I take this to be a reference to E. A. Robinson, who is otherwise without mention in the first period of Brooks.) There is no awareness whatever of the literature of interior or frontier America. There is no awareness of a rich New England literature which exists apart from the classics and which Mr. Brooks had to take into account when he came to write *The Flowering of New England* and *New England: Indian Summer*. Except for a few generalizations about oratory, which seem to refer to Daniel Webster's speeches and the sermons of Puritan divines, there is no awareness of political literature. Social literature is exclusively Henry George. Satire does not exist beyond *The Biglow Papers,* and Franklin is merely the author of *Poor Richard's Almanack* — a Philistine who, it develops, co-operated with the Puritans to give America its base commercial philosophy.

Let me repeat. Mr. Brooks set out to judge our society by means of literature and nothing else. Moreover, he limited literature to belles-lettres. (*The Federalist* is outside literature, whether by definition or by ignorance, and so are Jefferson, Calhoun, Lincoln, all the historians, all the educators, all the agitators, all the reformers, and all but two of the editors.) And finally, his knowledge of the literature to which he limited himself was fragmentary and superficial. In all these respects, the other leading literary thinkers of the 1920's were to follow his example — and also in one more respect which must be pointed out. In his description of life and literature in America Mr. Brooks was repeatedly to make statements for which he had the warrant of no knowledge whatever.[4]

Confidently, debonairly, sweepingly, and with a finality that permitted neither exception nor appeal, he was to assert as true of American history, literature, thought, and the details of our institutions, traditions and ways of living together — he was to assert as true, statements of a kind which only one who knew these things thoroughly would be entitled to make at all but which revealed that he had not bothered to find out anything about them. He arrived at them by intuition, by axiom, by consulting his emotions, by deducing specific instances from general principles, or by logically working out what must be true. These assertions were fundamental in what he said about America. They were accepted as the basis of what many other writers had to say about America in the generation that followed. They were subjective statements of private sentiments — but they were accepted as objective descriptions of historical facts.

Coming to the writers by whom he is to judge society, Mr. Brooks soon finds that they were unimportant. They were unimportant because their ideas were trivial. When he explains their triviality he runs to contradictions — his complaint is miscellaneous rather than coherent. He repeatedly assails the writers who composed the flowering of New England for not rigorously holding to artistic (by which he means esthetic) values, for corrupting artistic values with religious, ethical, or moral values. He asserts and repeatedly implies that literature must be dedicated solely to artistic (esthetic) values. Nevertheless, while holding it to be a serious fault of these writers that they expressed the values of their society, he repeatedly rebukes them for not holding firmly to social values. This ambivalence or confusion, however, is resolved when it becomes clear what he means by social values. Thus, after saying that James Russell Lowell wasted his talents, he speaks of "The Commemoration

Ode" and *The Biglow Papers* and goes on to say: "Slavery and the Mexican War receive in *The Biglow Papers*, it seems to me, just the right measure of literary attention; and this is a felicity which, in the light of his general exuberance, powers of expression, strength and solidity, makes one feel that he could have risen aptly to issues of a more strictly social type had they existed in his background."

This is a revealing pronouncement. "Just the right measure" and "felicity" are somewhat disparaging expressions; they suggest that literature was justified in paying some attention to slavery and the Mexican War but must be on its guard not to overemphasize them. (War and freedom must not distract us from esthetics, perhaps.) But observe the altogether astonishing remark that, if only they had existed in his background, Lowell might have *risen* to issues of *a more strictly social type.* Biographical ignorance is at maximum; any knowledge whatever of Lowell's experience and background would have prevented such a remark. As for social background: in writing about that period of American history one is required to know that it had to face three social issues of overwhelming importance, of importance so great that the nature and even the existence of society depended on them — slavery, developing industrialism, and the expansion of our national domain. One is required to know that the Mexican War involved all three and brought the first and third to climax. One is required to know that their interaction in the Mexican War made inevitable the most tremendous disaster of our history, the Civil War, and that they therefore changed the structure and pattern of American life. Mr. Brooks did not require himself to know such things and no one else required him to. Disregarding innumerable issues of reform with which Lowell occupied himself, thinking only of the supreme issues of his generation, one wonders what an issue "of a more strictly social type" would be. Then one finds out, for presently it becomes clear that by "social issue" Mr. Brooks means literary issue.[5] He understands society as literature.

After briefly characterizing and rebuking a number of our writers, after making many true statements and a great many false statements about them,[6] Mr. Brooks finally absolves them. It is true that they are trivial. But they had no chance. There can be great writers only in a great society and that, he proceeds to make clear, their America assuredly was not.

There follows a description of American life, past and present, more detailed than the characterization of writers but no less confused. Contemporary American culture has "a final unreality" but that is only the fated harvest of an unhappy sowing. "The Puritan Theocracy is the all-influential fact in the history of the American mind." A "centrifugal expediency" has always characterized every aspect of our life, prohibiting "centrality in thought" and "common standards of any kind." (But a little later it is to come out that we are culturally homogeneous and that an iron uniformity has always been imposed on all our thinking and beliefs.) Our language, our education, and our thought are either unreal or vulgar; our life splits into barren intellectuality or mere commerce. The ends of our society are impersonal and therefore we have never had personality.[7] Mr. Brooks is hopelessly ambivalent about one fundamental attribute of America. He oscillates between asserting that whereas individualism is the most seemly goal of effort the whole force of our culture has always prevented Americans from developing it, and asserting that an infrangible, commercially determined, fiercely self-protective individualism has always prevented them from achieving the most seemly goal of effort, which is a collective life. In general Americans have never developed personality, or tried to express it in their work, or been permitted to express it. America is provincial, bourgeois (in the Flaubertian, not the Marxian sense), and therefore hostile to men of talent. We are a business civilization.

This last is the master truth from which our baseness stems. Mr. Brooks never achieves a clear idea of Calvinism. But he identifies Calvinism as Puritanism, with that term he gives the 1920's their supreme eidolon, and he holds it responsible for all our offenses.[8] Puritanism, he says, was sharply divided into a doctrinal metaphysics and a philosophy of action. The first was rigorously confined to Sunday sermons and the world beyond the grave. The second unified, energized, and justified the unlovely American personality in its sole activity, the pursuit of wealth. Thus Puritanism showed itself a superb, in fact an indispensable, instrument for the spoliation of our wilderness continent. To the single end, acquisitiveness, it sacrificed all the graces of life, and not only the graces but even the realities. It gave Americans their notable contempt for emotion — in fact for all experiences except that of material gain.[9] It deprived them of all sense of the community and so forbade collective life to exist. It made them contemptuous of ideals, and the ambition of every American boy has always been to become the owner of a shoe factory. It withered their roots, it deprived them of mellowness, spirituality, and appreciation of life's warmth and vividness, and in fact of everything that can reasonably be called civilization. It made their intellectual life unreal and abstract, it confined their science to mere invention, and — first, last, and always — it denied them art. There have been no great artists in America, no great leaders, no great men.[10]

I have been reproducing the argument of *America's Coming-of-Age*. Toward the end of that book two things become evident. Mr. Brooks's assessment of American culture is oriented from two monuments: he has a theory about the ideal functions of writers in society, and he has a much wider acquaintance with European literatures than with American literature. They overlap but the first is the most important force in his rejection of American society and the second the most important force in his rejection of American literature.

To state now what is not fully stated till later in Mr.

Brooks's writing, his theory about the function of writers is a form of the assumption with which he began his appraisal of America: the measure of a culture is its literature. Writers have a threefold function: to serve as the standard of value of their culture, to appraise society by passing judgments of value on it, and to lead society. Just what he means by the cultural or social leadership (he uses the adjectives interchangeably) of writers is exceedingly difficult to arrive at, because here his thinking is irradiated with rhetoric and because he frequently contradicts himself.[11] It may be said, however, that he desires writers to be an Academy. Naturally the Academy shall have final jurisdiction over esthetic matters and questions of taste. But also it shall be the custodian of all other cultural values, and it shall be charged with authority over the ideals and aspirations of society and the national myths, aims, and goals. It shall not only express and appraise them, it shall determine what they are to be. Furthermore, society shall acknowledge the Academy's authority and shall obey its decrees. Finally, though this becomes clear only gradually and is only in part explicit, the Academy shall, in the name of all this authority, exercise leadership in practical affairs, politics, legislation, justice, and the ordinary conduct of public and private life.

Now if any society in history has ever granted such authority to its literary men, clearly American society has never done so. That, precisely, is the basis of Mr. Brooks's impeachment of American society.

Moreover, Mr. Brooks's knowledge of European literatures makes him refer to them, as criteria, the failures which he perceives in American literature. His references are to Goethe, Heine, Nietzsche, Tennyson, Carlyle, Matthew Arnold, William Morris, H. G. Wells, and presently Flaubert, other French writers, and the great Russian novelists. He constantly censures American writers for not being so great as these foreign writers are. Though his impression of their social leadership is essentially romantic, he is unobjectionable when he reproaches American literature for not being their equivalent.[12] But presently he is censuring American literature for not being the same as European literature. And with that censure the theoretical structure of his first period is completed.

His criticism is now seen to be abstract, deductive, contradictory, unsupported by fact, not derived from either the literature or the society it discusses, and what logicians call argument in a circle. There are no great American writers because American society is not great, and the proof that American society is not great is that it has produced no great writers. The central failure of our writers comes from their flaccid willingness merely to express our culture, but their central failure is a result of their being cut off from our culture. Our greatest need is to develop a native literature which shall express our native life, but on the one hand we have no native life, and on the other hand writers who express our native life growing from native roots are at fault for not having produced a literature like that of England, France, or Russia. This last dilemma, phrased first in general terms, becomes, as Mr. Brooks's books go on, a specific objection to many writers. In theory he passionately desired a native American literature, but when he had to deal with one it distressed him because it was not like European literature. One horn of the dilemma led to his fundamental misconception of Mark Twain,[18] the other to his rejection of Henry James. It was wrong of James to try to be Balzac, and it was wrong of Mark Twain not to try to be Dostoievsky. But for both wrongs American culture was to blame.

Clearly this criticism carried within itself the seeds of inevitable frustration. It did not originate in reality and it failed to make contact with reality.

All these ideas were present in his book of 1915. From then on, through *Letters and Leadership*, *The Ordeal of Mark Twain*, and *The Pilgrimage of Henry James*, they were developed and proliferated. The attack turned away from writers and concentrated on American society, which came to be regarded essentially (if not indeed solely) as a culture that poisoned literature at its source. (Mr. Brooks bore in mind that he was using the word "conspiracy" figuratively. In time, however, his followers were to speak of a "conspiracy against the good life" as literally as a later literary coterie spoke of "the capitalist conspiracy.") The allegations became more sweeping, more violent, more contradictory, more hysterical — and more ignorant. Mr. Brooks was presently talking about personifications and abstractions to the exclusion of objective facts, he was analyzing exclusively by means of syllogisms that arose out of earlier syllogisms and ended in other syllogisms. The result was that, whatever the truth about American life may be, it went disregarded in a rapt vision that grew steadily more like a nightmare.

"Morbid, bloodless, death in life" — we begin to get that kind of epithet describing America.[14] *The Spoon River Anthology* is the "inner life of a typical American community." Those identical twins the Puritan and the Pioneer have done for us and we never have had a civilization, a living culture, a culture which released the creative energies of men. On behalf of our barren culture the function of our literature has always been to anesthetize us so that we might conduct the repulsive frenzy of the acquisitive life untroubled by conscience. "We have no national fabric of spiritual experience." [15] In fact we have no experience at all in any worthy sense. The acquisitive life has established a rigid taboo against experience, has forbidden it to exist. Everything is repressed that might interfere with the material efficiency of the environment, and the environment is denatured, stripped of everything that might nourish the imagination. Imagination can seldom appear in a race specialized as Puritan-Pioneers; but when it does appear, self-protective fury maims or kills it. Because we have no belief in experience we habitually repress the creative spirit, and so we have no creative conception of life and no

fund of spiritual experience in our blood. . . . Therefore, as another avenue of approach has demonstrated,
we get no artists, no writers. But artists are the measure
of things.

Nevertheless we are going to get that measure, and
this whole denunciation of American life is felt as a
summons or challenge to writers. Writers are to be our
"awakeners." They are to break our trance, refine away
our dross, purge us of unworthiness and evil and Philistinism and materialism and the profit system, bind us
together in the collective life we have never had, give
us grace and thoughtfulness and health and spirituality,
exorcise the Puritan and Pioneer, vitalize our experience,
lead us to the great society and at last, after three centuries of sin and shame, teach us to walk the earth as
poets do. There can be no hope for America unless
writers become leaders of our national life, but the great
day when they will become leaders is now at hand. In
the movement of which he is a part Mr. Brooks perceives
the stirring, the Newness. A new literary generation has
been born, writers less magisterial than those of the older
day but more hard-minded, deep-seeking, obstinate, and
courageous, writers who are determined to give America
a soul. The old traditions and repressions are broken, the
old timidities and compromises are ended, the new assessment is under way. From Mr. Brooks's contemporaries
and their successors we are likely to get what we have
never had before, a great literature, and therefore a great
national life. The Academy is going to assert its au-

thority, its authority is going to be acknowledged, and writers will be leaders at last.[16]

One may say of these critical ideas elaborated into a system that they are young, hopeful, and passionately felt. One must say that they are generously intended, they arise from a hot desire that life and literature in America may be nobler than they have been. They express a fierce idealism which desires to keep America faithful to its promise, to correct the abuses, right the injustices, and root out the venalities and mediocrities of our national life, as well as to make our literature a splendid force in the world.

But one must also say of these ideas that they fail altogether to be what they set out to be, a description of America, a search for a "usable past." In the circumstances no outcome except total failure was possible. The inevitability of their failure lay first in ignorance and second in the assumptions behind them and the method of approach. Mr. Brooks simply did not know the American past or American literature, and one who is reasonably well acquainted with either is constantly agape at his page by page, even sentence by sentence falsification. By what warrant, one is continually asking, by what arrogance or blind folly, does a critic who obviously has never inquired into his subject-matter presume to manufacture judgment out of ignorance? Has there not been left out of the critical process the indispensable first step without which criticism cannot possibly make sense?

Yet, though ignorance of factual realities must vitiate

any analysis, and vitiates this one, it is the lesser error, for simple study could correct it. When at the age of forty-five [17] Mr. Brooks got round to reading the literature on the basis of which he had previously condemned our culture, he did amend a vast amount of earlier misrepresentation. The hopeless error is not ignorance but the method of approach. That method is the method of abstract, deductive reasoning, anchored not in objective and verifiable realities but in general principles, proceeding under no factual control, out of purely theoretical assertions, by way of purely theoretical observations, to purely theoretical conclusions. It is a complex organization of prepossessions, assumptions, arguments, errors, and emotions — a dynamism which I have here chosen to call the literary fallacy.

Reduced to general terms, the literary fallacy assumes: that a culture may be understood and judged solely by means of its literature, that literature embodies truly and completely both the values and the content of a culture, that literature is the highest expression of a culture,[18] that literature is the measure of life, and finally that life is subordinate to literature.

Later on I shall mention certain psychological implications of this fallacy. But something else must now be said about the ideas which I have been summarizing.

For those ideas fell on soil well prepared by events, changes, and developments of the preceding twenty years in America to make them germinate. As the 1920's came on, the literary scene, like the social scene, was

lively, exuberant, experimental, and charged with energy
at a high potential. There was, or seemed to be, a new
generation of writers, energetic, genially irreverent,
skeptical, inquiring, vastly interested, and (for many
reasons) freer, more sanctioned, more respected, and
more widely listened to than writers had been in America for some time. They already had (if only half-consciously) the praiseworthy intention to sift and analyze
American life, explore our past, assess and reassess it.
Those writers had recommended to them, at the high
level of Mr. Brooks's talent and sincerity, certain findings and certain methods which they adopted and proceeded to apply.

I remind you that I have limited my subject matter.
I am not trying to tell you about all the literature of the
1920's but about one aspect only of it, and especially
about one way of thinking about America. The main
current of American literature of the 1920's adopted Mr.
Brooks's findings (some of which it was approaching in-
dependently) and his method (which is, of course, a traditional method of literary thinking) — adopted them
completely, enthusiastically, as a revelation of unchal-
lengeable truth, and with no sense whatever that if submitted to the realities for which they had been substituted
they might collapse altogether. They were incorporated
in what may be called literature's official literature of the
1920's. Since they were the sincere expression of a distinguished talent, they became the most fruitful ideas of
that literature. Mr. Brooks had either originated for the

official literature or had supported with the period's finest talent, various key ideas, methods, and judgments.

It would be easy to specify individual ideas either originated by Mr. Brooks for his contemporaries or firmly established for them by his authority. Thus Mr. Waldo Frank learned or was confirmed in his belief that Americans were a people dominated by fear, without capacity for joy, and murderously hostile to beauty and wholeness and oneness. (The Indians excepted, or at least those within an easy day's drive of Santa Fe.) Mr. Lewis Mumford (together with many others) had demonstrated for his guidance that a historian may recover the American past by merely thinking about it, restoring the actual dinosaur by meditating on an abstract vertebra or a purely theoretical tooth. Mr. Ludwig Lewisohn was sanctioned to seek the entire explanation of a society which he found altogether loathsome in the Puritan's fear and hatred of sex. Through these critics and others of like mind, building houses of thought with Mr. Brooks's bricks, innumerable playwrights and novelists were told that we were a Puritanical, materialistic, acquisitive people, without personality, of base ideals, unlovely in our private and public life, inhibited in emotion, uniform in thought, mediocre, dull, dreary, and base.[19] Innumerable literary thinkers preparing to investigate our past were told that it was the repulsive history of a few evil forces working among a simple, homogeneous people who had no culture, in the service of base ends, as the enemies of enlightenment, beauty, and even life itself. Mr. H. L. Mencken received support from an unexpected source — one which could not have greatly comforted him — for the idea which he had been joyfully developing, that the Europeans who had committed the folly of crossing the Atlantic were an inferior breed, whose chromosomes necessarily perpetuated inferiority among their progeny. Thinkers of a more political cast of mind now had literary support for theories of sovereignty which assumed that the people were fools and that the institutions of a foolish people must be corrupt and contemptible.

Not the specific findings concern us now, however, but the principle in action. Writers had been told that the Americans were an inferior people, that America was not a worthy subject of art, that America was in fact hostile to art, and that the artist as American was a figure of tragic frustration. They had been shown by brilliant example that literary thinking need not consult realities and requires no objective control, no control at all beyond that of logic, that the reality killeth whereas the theory giveth life, that the truth about America is recoverable by a private search of the writer's soul. More important still, they had been told that literary ideas should be the final basis of cultural judgments, that literature is the most important activity of society, that writers either are or of right ought to be the leaders of society, and that a society in which they are not leaders is base.

Most important of all was a result which Mr. Brooks did not cause by precept or example but which was necessarily conditioned and produced by his conception of writers. He desired writers to be an Academy which would at once crown, judge, and lead a great society. With the intensity of a passionate nature he desired writers to create a finer national life which it would then be their duty to express. It did not work out that way. It worked out far otherwise, though in a still logical and logically predictable way. For, if literature is the highest aim of culture, and if the American people were inferior and their culture barren, base, and hostile to literature — then what was the use? If American culture would not constitute its writers an Academy — then it became inevitable, a merely mechanical reaction, for writers to constitute themselves a special and superior caste.

That is precisely what literature's official literature in the 1920's proceeded to do. Mr. Brooks had felt in his contemporaries, so he thought, the stirrings of a great and fruitful affirmation. But what they proceeded to work out was, instead, the repudiation of American life in witness of which I have quoted Mr. Brooks and Mr. MacLeish. That repudiation was conducted on many levels, from Mr. Brooks's pure and passionate sincerity, down through the merely fashionable, the merely flip, or the merely vulgar, to the cheaply sensational and deliberately dishonest. For the vulgarization of his ideas, for cheap exhibitionism and careless lying and stupid charlatanism — all of which were sometimes granted validity in that official repudiation — he can in no way be held responsible. Moreover what I have described

as the literary fallacy, which is the medium his work
exists in, is not the sole force in the literary repudiation
of American experience. But it is by far the most important force, and more than anyone else, though on the
highest level, he gave it generative power in the literature of the 1920's. It is, essentially, the belief that literature is the measure of culture.

1. The break appears to have come when Mr. Brooks began to read Emerson seriously and discovered in him almost exactly the kind of writer he had rebuked America for not producing.

2. Many writers who shared the effort sincerely believed that no such description and appraisal had ever been attempted before.

3. They antedated the literary awareness of Melville. At least two of Melville's books, *Typee* and *Omoo*, had never been out of print — or rather had periodically been reprinted. American boys had always read them as adventure books, and they and *Moby Dick* had long had an adult audience in England. There had always been, as well, a small number of enthusiasts, some of them literary critics, who had revered Melville's work and kept his reputation alive, though they had made it a rather esoteric reputation. It was their preparation to commemorate his centennial in 1919 that called him to the attention of literary people at large. By that time the movement of which Mr. Brooks's ideas were a part had progressed so far that Melville instantly became a symbol. Literary opinion seized on him as a type-specimen of the artists who had been frustrated by the materialism and conformity of American life, and for ten years no one bothered to say much else about him. Even now there is no really good biography of him, and though there are excellent short psychological and critical studies of his books no one has undertaken to free him from the clichés of the Twenties.

"Had he heard of Emily Dickinson?" Mr. Brooks asks, concerning George Woodberry, in his second period. (He had not heard of her when he found our literature trivial.) "Had he heard of Melville? He had small use for Whitman, and Mark Twain, Howells, and James meant little to him.

This literature had wholly 'failed to establish an American tradition' and it had failed to produce a poet 'even of the rank of Gray.'" (*Indian Summer*)

4. In some departments of the intellectual life this would be an extremely serious accusation. One must understand at the very beginning, however, that it is not a serious or even a relevant accusation according to the way of thinking which these lectures examine. In that way of thinking the criterion of an idea is its rightness as idea, not the knowledge which it represents or its correspondence to reality. The method of literary thinking proceeds from idea to idea by way of idea, with no check or control outside idea. It deduces ideas from assumptions, general principles, and universal abstract truths. It requires facts to conform to logic and it ascertains facts by determining what logic implies.

When I first made this accusation, in *Mark Twain's America*, certain critics indignantly rebuked me. Not being able to answer for Mr. Brooks, I could only say that he had made many statements which so intelligent a man could not possibly have made if he had read the books or looked up the facts he was talking about — if, that is, he considered that the facts had any bearing on his statements. Since then Mr. Brooks has confirmed what I said. "He [Oliver Allston, Mr. Brooks's literary projection of himself] had ridiculed Emerson, Longfellow, Whittier, and Bryant . . . nor did he regret this, although he regretted now and then that he had not really read these poets first. He had not really read them for he was too impatient with them, but it would not have changed his feeling if he had read them. . . ." (*Opinions of Oliver Allston*, 192–193) Similar comments, which are not felt to be admissions, are made several times in the book.

5. Precisely the same disparagement weakens his treatment of Thoreau in *The Flowering of New England*.

6. Together with many flashes of brilliant insight such as

occur repeatedly in all his books. They show Mr. Brooks's talent at its best but they tend to be discrete — of the immediate context only, frequently irrelevant to the general argument, sometimes contradictory of it. Some of the things he says about Hawthorne in *America's Coming-of-Age*, for instance, are so fine that the wonder is they did not altogether amend his characterization of Hawthorne and thus refute the argument rested on it.

7. The assertion that Americans lack personality is twinned with the uniformity formula. Both are fixed clichés in the literature of the Twenties, articles of the Literary Credo which George Jean Nathan never got round to publishing as an appendix to *The American Credo*. In spite of its importance in the system, however, few writers ever tried to explain what they meant by personality and the student is left to the dangerous expedient of inference. To Sinclair Lewis personality seems to have meant archness, that curiously inane glibness of women disenchanted with housekeeping and men grown too wise for belief in Rotary which was supposed to be altogether different from the talk of drummers in smoking cars. Mencken's ideas were more complex but, at a guess, personality meant to him primarily an interest in chamber music. Some writers clearly meant dress reform, others a public advertisement of their sexual experience, others folk dancing or its equivalent in economics. Harold Stearns lights up at least a quarter of the whole literature when he explains that ugliness in France has a "lift" that it lacks in America. One approaches a generalization: usually personality is not positive but negative, it is something else that Americans lack, but it involves an ability to discuss literary ideas.

There appears to be a sustained effort to explain the meaning of personality in Floyd Dell's *Intellectual Vagabondage* but it fails and one concludes that he meant the manners transiently practised by literary people in the society of Greenwich Village just before the First World War. This book is a tolerably complete statement of the Literary Credo, or at any rate a useful summary of the literary clichés accepted in the earliest part of our period, the innocent and hopeful years.

8. Puritanism was the fluid and multiform villain of the Twenties. Again, however, the student who tries to find out what the boys were talking about must work under discouraging handicaps. Many thousands of pages exposed the infinite indecencies, corruptions, and frustrations which Puritanism had inflicted on our civilization. But few of them tried to define or anatomize Puritanism and practically none tried to establish any relationship between the literary cliché and historical Puritanism. One can, however, reach a few reasonably clear conclusions. The largest category of offenses attributed to Puritanism by literary people (and practically all the offenses which Mencken, for instance, called Puritan) were in fact doctrines or practices of the evangelical sects — sects which the Puritan churches despised and fought, which arose as a rebellion against Puritanism, which throughout their history have warred against Puritanism in our culture. Perhaps the second largest category was shaped by a literary phantasy, a notion that Puritanism forbade, feared, and despised sexual intercourse, the emotions associated with it in personality, and the expression of such emotions in art. This leads to the establishment of another clear category of offenses: Puritanism's opposition to, prohibition of, and sustained war on all art, objects of art, music, singing, painting, and, most especially and personally, imaginative literature. Beyond this the cliché cannot be analyzed satisfactorily: Puritanism was just something to which you attributed whatever portions of our culture you happened to dislike.

Throughout this endless manipulation of a stereotype there is astonishingly little reference to historic Puritanism and astonishingly little awareness that the development of our culture has involved strains of thought and feeling different from Puritanism, at odds with it, or complementary to it. Moreover, it is extremely rare to find a literary crusader against Puritanism referring directly to historic Puritans, to Puritan texts, records, practices, or institutions, or to the process of change and transformation within Puritanism. Very few literary people ventured to impugn the cliché. Stuart Sherman made a notable protest, whose very heat is evidence of its singularity, and Mark and Carl Van Doren knew too much history and literature to yield to fashion, but most thinkers sailed with the wind. The literary fallacy makes the consultation of extra-literary phenomena unnecessary; the critics ignored objective studies of Puritanism which were being made by other hands even as they wrote and which shattered the literary cliché to its component idiocies. Thus in the early Twenties students of politics were completing a sound and comprehensive study of the influence of Puritanism in one area of our inheritance, completely unaware that the Puritans had effected three centuries of cultural bankruptcy, and the main current of historiography serenely continued its investigation of Puritanism unimpeded and uninvoked by literary people. Or almost unimpeded — for there was an occasional communication across the lines and the truth is that occasionally a historian was infected by the literary cliché. Thus Mr. James Truslow Adams has had to make a recantation similar to Mr. Brooks's. His early books have in some part been repealed by his later ones.

9. Bear in mind, however, that at need the system also represents the Americans as the most wildly and uncontrollably emotional of peoples.

10. Evidence for these assertions is never offered; they are hortatory. These things are so because Mr. Brooks knows they are so; he knows they are so because deduction from ineluctable axioms proves that they must be so. Details of the argument in a vacuum are fascinating but cannot be quoted at length. I insert just one of them. Mr. Brooks is speaking of New England at the period which he was later to call its flowering. He says, "Painting, sculpture, architecture were represented by engravings; history, travel, world-politics, great affairs in general were represented by books." (That is, the New Englanders feared experience, shunned it, and substituted lifeless representations of it in what passed as their culture.) At the precise time he is dealing with, New England dominated the carrying trade of the world, and its institutions and daily life were informed by a cosmopolitan experience more widespread and more thoroughgoing than any section of America has ever had since. Its great houses and its cottages were filled with what Mr. Mumford was soon to call the loot of Europe, and not only of Europe but of the Far East, the Middle East, and the Pacific islands as well. The line of Copley and Stuart was being continued by many painters whom Mr. Brooks was later to write about with great respect (after one of whom he was to name his projected self) and by humbler painters whom Constance Rourke was to discuss with his approval — not to mention the steady procession of Yankees to and from Italy, studying art, producing art, bringing art home, making it an integral part of their sectional culture. At that moment New England brought to another high expression, perhaps the highest expression, the domestic architecture which remains on the whole the finest that America has ever had — and which has not lacked praise from Mr. Brooks's coterie or in his later books. At that moment New England was developing the clipper ship, the

most beautiful of all objects which American artists have ever made, a complete expression of the esthetic function in vocation which Mr. Brooks flatly denied us. The great scholars and historians were busy at their jobs, with great work done and great work ahead of them. Yankee politicians were — not for the first time — remaking the domestic and foreign policies of the United States, were helping to give the nation the place in world organization which it maintained throughout the nineteenth century. In "great affairs" Yankee business men, industrialists, financiers, colonizers, agitators, reformers, speculators, scientists, and educators were remaking the nation — and so were remaking the world.

What is the point? Why not simply remark that this sort of thing is merely the exuberance of a young man laying about him with an enjoyment which his readers may share? Why not simply point out that this is young Greenwich Village of 1915 with its collar unbuttoned and must not be taken seriously? The point is that it was taken seriously. Mr. Brooks did not bother to consult the facts, to stand on the realities. He did not know what he was talking about. He presumed to make judgments which were in fact ignorant and false. He used those judgments, and others used them, in the co-operative literary effort to describe America. He was wrong and those who used his findings were wrong. This is one specimen of the literary misrepresentation of American life.

11. Thus he repeatedly says that writers cannot properly have any direct interest whatever in society but also repeatedly says that society must be their central subject. Writers cannot be concerned with morality but also they must supply the moral content of a culture. Writers can have nothing to do with rebellion but they must constantly destroy the old forms of life and provide new ones.

12. Though sometimes absurd. "This open, skeptical,

sympathetic centrality of theirs [Englishmen in touch with English writers] articulates the whole life of the people, and incidentally as a matter of course expresses itself through legislation. More than one English book by an unknown writer has, within two years and owing to this diffused sense of the hierarchy of ideas, penetrated Parliament, convinced it, and been at once translated into action." . . . "Carlyle counts his disciples from generation to generation; strong men and leaders of men, they go out conquering and ruling creation, and there is hardly a British governor who does not feel upon his head the apostolic hands of Carlyle." . . . "In Europe, where the warfare of ideas, of social philosophies, is always an instant close-pressed warfare in which everyone is engaged, Lowell would have had an opportunity to bring his artillery into play. In America, where no warfare of ideas has ever existed, where ideas have always been acutely individual and ethical, and where public and social affairs, disjointed and vague, have always met with the yawning indifference that springs from a relative want of pressure behind, he inevitably became indifferent." . . . I call attention to the simple and superb statement that no warfare of ideas has ever existed in America. I, for one, do not understand why any argument based on such an understanding should ever have been taken seriously by anyone. But though it is fundamental in Mr. Brooks's system and though it represents an ignorance of our past absolutely paralyzing to good sense, it is nevertheless a passionate idealism with him and therefore in an odd way to be respected, whereas, taken over whole and elaborated by other hands, it became contemptible in much of the writing of the Twenties.

13. Analyzed in my *Mark Twain's America*. Note, moreover, that part of his distaste for Mark Twain was a simple uneasiness in the presence of humor which can be observed throughout his work. In all his books the only humor which

does not in some way disturb him is *The Peterkin Papers* —
an extremely revealing fact.

Permit me a personal note. Having attacked Mr. Brooks's
ideas in one book, I was reluctant to attack them again
in this one. I spent some months carefully reading all the
books of his coterie in the hope of centering this examination of the period on someone else. The reason which had
proved conclusive fifteen years ago, however, proved conclusive again: I could not find anyone else whose ideas were
as intelligent, integrated, central, and influential as his. He
was not only the leader of the movement, he was its best
mind.

14. But "Europe is alive in all its members; in its lone-
liest and most isolated corner there is hardly a hamlet where
life does not still persist, as green and warm and ruddy as the
heart of an old apple tree."

15. There is a curious continuity in Mr. Brooks, a central ignorance or a central misunderstanding, which is common to the entire movement. He repeatedly attacks the very
thing which he also says America lacked altogether; he
specifically laments the absence of things which he rebukes
us for having. He, with his entire school, failed to see that
the establishment on this continent of new hopes and op-
portunities and ways of life, the enhancement of human
expectation, the democratization of society, the development
of democratic government, the expansion of the frontier, the
adventure of opening and occupying a continent, the adaptation of Europeans to novel conditions of life which produced "the American, this new man," the evolution of a
native culture, the accretion of an American society — he
failed to see that such things were in fact what he re-
proached us for not having, a national fabric of spiritual
experience. Our spiritual experience was different from
Europe's — that was the fact behind his perception. But from

that perception followed two findings: that therefore it was an inferior spiritual experience, and that therefore we had no spiritual experience at all. From that point on his system, or the system of his followers, could use either finding as the occasion might require. That simple logical process produced much harmless nonsense and much dangerous nonsense in the literature of the 1920's.

Mr. Brooks was to write, later on, "The real experience of the country, which found a voice in literature, was vague and repugnant to [Barrett] Wendell. And naturally he was half-hearted, therefore, even about its greatest writers, even in his own New England, to say nothing of the rest." Here, as in many other passages of the later books, Mr. Brooks makes an apt comment on himself.

16. Thus *Letters and Leadership*. It was published in 1918. A later, dissenting fashion in literary opinion held that the First World War broke the movement off short. Quite the contrary. When the war was ending Mr. Brooks felt the movement as just beginning to gather momentum.

This book did, however, mark the crest of Mr. Brooks's optimism. By *The Ordeal of Mark Twain* he was willing to disavow in their entirety our past, what he held to be our traditions, and the intellectual and emotional content of our culture. Considering the past, there could be no hope at all. The epithets became more blasting — see, for example, the famous "desert of human sand" passage. The twinned eidolons, Puritan and Pioneer, became more hideously destructive. The generalizations became more absolute.

Neither *The Ordeal of Mark Twain* nor *The Pilgrimage of Henry James* added much that was new to the edifice of Mr. Brooks's ideas. By this time, however, he had resolved one contradiction. Individualism, instead of being a powerful and evil force which the ruthlessly self-minded Puritan-Pioneer had exerted to prevent the development of a common life, was now seen to be what Americans lacked most completely, something which the Puritan-Pioneer would not permit to exist at all, fearing it and ruthlessly suppressing every effort to develop or express it. The Puritan-Pioneer's suppression of individualism was what had produced the dreary uniformity of thought, emotion, behavior, and belief that extended across all the American past and the American present. Likewise it was what had killed art, for art — by this time — must be understood as individualism.

Another basic idea had been somewhat transformed. The barrenness and unreality of American experience were now interpreted as resulting from the inability of Americans to experience joy, love, and all other expansive emotions. This striking inability proved us to be a people suspicious and even fearful of pleasure, unable to laugh, not gifted at satire, dominated by dourness and even depression. This idea that we are an unemotional people (or a people who inhibit emotion) joined with the idea that we are also a people stamped into uniformity to heighten to fatuous absurdity the general idea that the American environment is and always has been unfavorable to artists. The environment is unfavorable to artists and we have no joyful experiences — consequently there is in America no material fit for art to treat. The sentiment was constant but it had found a new rationalization: previously what had frustrated the artist was the active hostility of the environment, but now it was the simple unfitness of the environment. It was not so much that artists were defeated as that they withered in poisoned soil. This led to Mr. Brooks's report that America had never had any of the rich humus of folk art from which a genuine art might perhaps have arisen at the command of awakeners. When a revised edition of *The Ordeal of Mark Twain* was published, the revision consisted of leaving out the assertion that we had no folk art.

17. Named in *The Opinions of Oliver Allston* as the age at which Mr. Brooks found out what he wanted to do.

18. In at least one passage of *Letters and Leadership* Mr. Brooks undertakes to show that literature not only is the highest goal which a culture can have but one to which it ought consciously to make tributary all the rest of its content.

19. Thus, at the moment when he was preparing to write about what he called the Village Virus, Mr. Sinclair Lewis could read: "It is the American village that most betrays the impulse of our civilization, a civilization that perpetually overreaches itself only to be obliged to surrender again and again to nature everything it has gained. How many thousand villages, frostbitten, palsied, full of a morbid, bloodless, death-in-life, villages that have lost, if they ever possessed, the secret of self-perpetuation, lie scattered across the continent! . . . I suppose it is only natural in the West. [As late as *Indian Summer* Mr. Brooks is still using the phrase "the West" not as a geographical expression but as an epithet] . . . [But] what shocks one is to realize that our Eastern villages, the seats of all the civilization we have [*sic*, and consult *Main Street*], are themselves scarcely anything but the waste and ashes of pioneering, and that no inner fire has taken possession of the hearth where the original flame so long since burned itself out."

On the same page, Mr. Eugene O'Neill might read, though the specific reference was to Long Island villages: "The crazy, weather-beaten houses that hold themselves up among their unkempt acres with a kind of angular dignity, the rotting porches and the stench of decay that hangs about their walls, the weed-choked gardens, the insect-ridden fruit trees, the rusty litter along the roads, the gaunt, silent farmers who stalk by in the dusk—how overwhelmingly they seem to betray a losing fight against the wilderness."

But, in *Indian Summer:* "as long as she [Miss Wilkins]
wrote in terms of the village, she possessed the village integrity and all the grand inheritance of the Puritan faith [!];
and this gave her a profundity that made her point of view,
at moments, all but universal."

III

The House of the Interpreter

THE preceding lecture examines the early books of Mr. Van Wyck Brooks as a statement of the general ideas that loosely united a sizable literary movement. It is interested in them as a method and a system, a way of thinking. This lecture begins with Mr. Brooks's later books. They represent, so to speak, a change of phase. They are radically different from the earlier books in intention, mood, and temper. They are frequently at odds with the earlier books, frequently contradict them, and come to an exact reversal of judgment. Nevertheless, there is a continuity between the two periods. Something which appears to be constant dominates both, and the reason for going on with Mr. Brooks instead of shifting the analysis to other writers is that by studying this continuity we can chart final limitations of what I have chosen to call the literary fallacy.

We are chiefly concerned with two books, *The Flowering of New England*, published in 1936, and *New England: Indian Summer*, published in 1940. They are the second and third volumes of a history of American literature which, we are told, Mr. Brooks hopes to complete in five volumes, the first, fourth, and fifth being as yet unpublished. Various critics have made various objections to them, but I think it would be generally agreed that, on the whole, they are the best studies of New England literature ever written. Most critics, in fact, would go farther than that. "Literary climate" is a phrase of critical shorthand which stands for the moods and feelings and ideas of writers, the ways in which books are conceived and the daily excitements in which they are written, for literary associations, literary experience, the tones and shade and nuances and colorations of writers' minds in relation to their books and to literature in general — in short, for the whole sum of literary affect and effect. Surely these two books are the best American study of literary climate, the best history of books we have. They are a mature expression of Mr. Brooks's distinguished talent. They are informed with the delight of a mind that has found its occupation and has mastered its material. They contain a great many truths and true judgments, passages profoundly understanding, passages justly and permanently interpretative — so many that I ask you to take them for granted.

But also they reveal fixed limitations imposed by the way of thinking which I have called the literary fallacy.

I have already suggested the first thing which must be said of them — and which might be said in greater detail than I have space for. The first of them throughout its length and the second very frequently retract, step by step, specifically, and almost in their entirety, statements about American life and American literature which had been fundamental in the theses out of which Mr. Brooks had written the books of his first period. These books were preceded, as the earlier ones were not, by a study of the writers they dealt with.[1] And when Mr. Brooks came to acquaint himself with his subject matter he found that it was not at all what his brilliant exercise in deductive logic had made it out to be.

He even found something of an Academy: writers who were arbiters at least of taste and literary opinion, who held in public esteem as high a place, or almost as high, as he believed writers ought to hold, in whose dignity the public took pride since it could be felt as a national dignity. He found that they were neither personally nor socially repressed but in fact spoke truly, confidently, and honorably for a vigorous common life of which they were an active part. He found them "awakeners" and at the same time he found that they expressed vigorous, vital traditions of their society. Moreover, he found that their society was a truly organic adaptation to its conditions, that it grew freely, powerfully, and even beautifully from native roots. Furthermore it truly contained a collective life — shared hopes, shared faiths, ideals, aspirations, and myths, common strengths, a common culture.

Many items of that earlier description were now reversed. Provincialism was gone altogether; Boston, Cam-

bridge, Concord, and their writers belonged to the great
world. They were, in fact, truly cosmopolitan since
they could bring to the great world a serene confidence
in their native experience. Neither Puritanism nor the
Puritan-Pioneer is an eidolon of negation or of fear.
Puritanism has become an exalted, dynamic religion
whose ecstatic spirituality is supported by a subtle intelligence. The Puritan has become the man who gave this
way of life its dignity. It is no longer a barren way of
life; the coarse, stripped villager has disappeared, and
so has the sterile dullness of his daily life. Instead, life
in this New England has grain, a sinewy and supple
richness, out of which come folk wisdom, folk thought,
folk poetry, and folk art to build up the humus for great
literature to grow in. We no longer hear of a people
whose will is to seek lifeless substitutes for reality. We
have a people who live deeply and express their life in
a culture the most genuine and various, through institutions which must be accorded a profound respect.

Furthermore, Mr. Brooks now permits culture and
literature wider boundaries than before. There is room
not only for universities but for museums and for
scholars, scientists, and mechanical craftsmen who in
the earlier period were either disregarded or dismissed
with a sneer. A politician like Daniel Webster, a
constitutionalist like Justice Story, a lawyer like Rufus
Choate, a mathematician like Nathaniel Bowditch, the
Yankee lexicographer Noah Webster, historians, social
reformers — Mr. Brooks's more catholic approach in-

cludes such people in the cultural tradition. It is, he makes clear, a great tradition. This is a self-respecting people. They live soundly, in a dignified consciousness, toward great ends. Their experience and their hope are real, and not only real but noble. And in their behalf literature, the literature which had previously been either nonexistent or contemptible, does what the vision of the young Brooks had desired literature always to do.

We cannot linger on this recantation. There is to be said of it that the facts had not changed in twenty years, and if what Mr. Brooks said of them in 1936 was true then what he said of them in 1915 was false. They had always been there and when he came to consult them he could use them in support of his judgments. But meanwhile for twenty years his false description had been a gospel to many writers whose careers consisted of preaching it to the dwellers in darkness. Mr. Brooks speaks of having conducted his education in public, but one might also say that he conducted it at the expense of the truth and it may be that he should have pointed a moral for young writers. Perhaps this is what Mr. MacLeish was talking about — perhaps there is a responsibility which writers should assume if a compliant public does not hold them to it. Perhaps part of that responsibility is that they should not conduct their education in public but should acquire education before presuming to educate others. Perhaps they should not try to tell the truth until they find out what it is, should not judge until they have qualified themselves for judgment. Lack of knowledge, however idealistic, remains ignorance. Misrepresentation, arising from whatever generosity of soul, is still falsehood. If much of the separation from American culture of an entire generation of writers can be explained as simple ignorance, easily reparable, it is not therefore any the less a separation. Mr. Brooks's ignorance was for years a public instrument of literature. With its aid many writers, sometimes with equally pure motives and frequently with greater positiveness, lied flatly about the people they were presuming to interpret.

Conceivably this is but a small damage. Certainly it is one which literary thinking can always avoid by finding out what it is talking about. Certainly also the damage to our culture was smaller than the damage to writers, for the irresponsibility of ignorance bred further irresponsibility. Given the sanction of a general description of America, and given a method which proceeded by consulting general principles without exterior control, it was possible to write criticism, history, and biography not only without reference to reality but without reference to common sense as well. If you could derive the general truths about American life by means of a purely logical process from purely theoretical tenets, then obviously you could derive any fact you might have use for by the same process from the same generalizations. If American experience in general was cheap, barren, and unreal, then any period or any person you might be interested in investigating must necessarily turn out to be a simple variation on the general theme. The reappraisal of American culture and the rewriting of American biography became a mere search for illustrations of the principles, a search which grew more vulgar and more dishonest. In the end it lost sight not only of the goal which it had set out for but also of the very past with which it had intended to deal on its way. A high intent degenerated to a mere fashion, the fashion was progressively debased, and it ended at last in pure boredom — the boredom of writers themselves. Ignorant, theoretical, and dishonest misrepresentations had submerged the American past so completely that new writers, coming to it afresh, honestly believed, as Mr. Brooks's coterie had believed in 1920, that they were the first writers who had ever undertaken to seek it out.[2]

The sense of history is so shockingly defective in Mr. Brooks and his followers that it cannot be completely explained as reparable ignorance — and so one turns to Mr. Brooks's mature books for light or leading. Looked at as a history of New England literature, they are seen to be extremely provincial in their understanding. Clearly Mr. Brooks is aware that the nation existed beyond the section, but only feeble, occasional implications of that existence cross an intangible barrier that walls it out. Sometimes — but tolerably seldom — he pays lip-service, usually in a single sentence which is not followed up, to national energies, currents, and issues. He will remark that the West was being settled, that new American adaptations were being worked out, that mills and factories were establishing new configurations of power, that conflicts on a national scale were being revealed. But such facts have little life for him and they do not affect the literary portraits he is drawing. Yet these are portraits of men who were violently affected by the facts that will not live for Mr. Brooks, men who dealt with those facts in their work much more centrally than he takes note of. The first of these books covers a period which marked New England's dominance and the beginning of its decline from national power. The decline of its cultural dominance, which is the theme of the second, cannot be separated from the decline of its power. The fact of its dominance gets occasional brief mention but exceedingly little is said about the nature of its power, apart from purely literary aspects of it. And a whole book studies the decline as weakening of literary belief and literary impulse.

That fact provides a clue. The clue shows more plainly when Mr. Brooks writes a chapter in *The Flowering* and half a chapter in *Indian Summer* [3] in which he is forced to deal with movements unmistakably national. In one he must confront abolitionism and in the other the transformation of the financial organization of the United States. It turns out that the first was a literary movement and the importance of the second was that it dismayed some literary men. Both are felt not as experience, not even as an experience out of which books arise, but exclusively as the writing of books. [4] Finally the clue becomes flagrant when one observes that *The Flowering* ends before the Civil War has begun and *Indian Summer* begins after it is finished. The Civil War does not exist in either book as a crucial, formative experience of an entire people. Such existence as it has is usually a sentence or two of allusion in what some writer has said about it — usually Henry Adams and therefore frequently wrong. Mr. Brooks has not been able to reduce it to a literary movement. One concludes that is why he cannot understand it.[5]

Moreover, even as forthrightly provincial history, these two books have astonishing limitations. They are, for instance, only in small part intellectual history. True, they include Channing and other divines, Ripley and other reformers, Agassiz and a few other scientists, Webster and Sumner, John Quincy Adams, William James, Clarence King. But though something is said about the importance of religious and political thinking, little vital relationship is established between such thinking and the life that conditioned it. The establishment of museums is chronicled, the existence of laboratories is at least acknowledged, but their intellectual function in the community is not appreciated. There is no sustained effort to chart, still less to appraise, the alteration of men's consciousness produced by scientific thought. Thinkers, whether scientific or social, are not people who develop out of and affect the common culture; they are people who observe literary traditions, who write books. Even the politicians, even the greatest Adams, who is specifically said to have had a socialistic vision, are primarily exponents of literary ideas. Webster and Sumner, who had a part in every violent social discord of their time, tend to become no more than stylists. The great historians are among Mr. Brooks's major characters and Prescott is one of his heroes, but not much is said in appraisal of their books and little or nothing is said about history as an embodiment of social experience. Prescott and Motley are literary figures. Bancroft is seriously misrepresented in that a judgment is passed on him which is essentially a literary snobbery.[6] Parkman is misconceived, and the lesser historians — some of whom faithfully reflected the national culture while others were so richly expressive of New England life that it has always had the best local history of all the sections — dwindle to mere literary antiquarians.

So it turns out that even during its flowering New England's principal energy was literary and even its decay was a decline of writers. Mr. Brooks refers to New England's base on the sea, but he does not study the economic and social integrations by means of which the sea wrought its effect on the Yankee imagination. The maritime industries as conditioning even exclusively cultural aspects of Yankee life go unstudied. We are not told how salt water created one strain of thinking in Yankee books but rather how literary men wrote beautifully about the sea.[7] He formally registers such things as the drainage westward of Yankee strength, the prominence of New Englanders in the development of the West, the acceleration of industrialism, and the increasing presence of Irish and other aliens. But these things are not seen as energies that shaped the life of individual and commonwealth alike, as experience vehement in the heart and decisive in personal destiny. They are mentioned and then dropped: Mr. Brooks is interested in showing us the delicacies of minds absorbed in the fascinating task of writing books.

There is an extended treatment of Brook Farm, a social experiment largely controlled by writers. But there is no understanding of the dislocation of familiar ways of life, no awareness of the desperation in the face of dimly understood, revolutionary new energies so powerful that they forced even writers to make social experiments. There is no mention of the much more intelligent communities in which realistic but unliterary persons actually tried to come to grips with the same problems. Those communities represented a basic strain in New England thought, New England dreaming, New England religion, and New England experience. The strain went back to the *Mayflower* and beyond. The communities were a profound experience to those who lived in them, they were an extremely important chapter of the nineteenth century in America, they left a permanent impression on the thought of the section, and they are in fact a part of our cultural inheritance. But they must be content to have existed without mention by Mr. Brooks, except that one of the groups who established communities, the Shakers, interested William Dean Howells and so has literary importance. Even Orestes Brownson is discussed without reference to the turbulence of which he was the first American writer to make an analysis that is still serviceable today. Even abolitionism is a force that produced books, not an energy of economic conflict or an episode in the war for human freedom.

Now this is an astonishing defect. It must be in part explained by an admission, which is equally astonishing, in *The Opinions of Oliver Allston:* —

> For years I was unable to interest myself in American history because of certain phrases that blocked my path. Whenever I opened Rhodes, for instance, I encountered one of these phrases that stood like sullen watch-dogs at the gate of the subject. "The resumption of specie payment" was one such phrase. What it means I know. . . . But the effort to associate . . . these meanings is too much for my mind . . . I do not wish to know too much about the "resumption of specie payment"; and I deprecate this phrase and the part it plays in every account of the age that preceded my own. . . . It made me feel that money questions dominated American history, and I was in revolt against money questions and the undue place they held in the national mind. It was largely for this reason that I could not enter American history. . . .

Thus Mr. Brooks himself tells us that what kept him from entering our history was a mere cliché stamped in Greenwich Village in its artiest days. Our past was full of money questions; money questions were vulgar and the good life could not take them into account. But obviously that does not tell the whole story. What is preventing Mr. Brooks from entering the American past is not only a cliché but a grave defect of imagination. He could not translate "the resumption of specie payments" into terms of national credit, the production of goods, the world flow of commerce, or even the warfare of parties, sections, and classes. He could not translate it into brownstone palaces on Murray Hill, endowments of Harvard College, or farmers dispossessed, corn burned for fuel, sons denied education, babies dying of malnutrition, night riders, a seething revolt of quite uncultivated people in graceless provinces to the westward — at the very moment when, in Mr. Brooks's book, nothing is being deeply felt in America because, consider, New England literature has been refined past vehemence. History would not live for him as human want and passion and despair in past time. And yet weakness of historical imagination obviously does not tell the full story, either. Mr. Brooks's indifference to history as historians wrote it found support in the literary fallacy. History must deal with the past of the literary life; it must think of the past as a time when writers now dead were writing books.

The Flowering of New England and New England: Indian Summer, then, are literary history conceived as the personal history of writers. Mr. Brooks once held literature to be a voice speaking for society but he does not write its history as such a voice. In order to be that kind of literary history, these books would have to be enlarged by other volumes which would take account of the life of New England that does not come between their covers and would relate the sum of that life to the life of the American people beyond the frontiers of Canaan.

Finally, one thinks, in order to recount the history of literature as in some way the equations of literature and life, they would have to have something else that they have not got.

For though one is delighted by many portraits and judgments, by many insights and explanations, by many passages where a sensitive talent gives us to the full all that can be asked of it, one also feels a recurring dissatisfaction. Surely, one thinks, surely So-and-so is but thinly conceived, or somewhat wronged, or seen only in part. Or surely So-and-so had more to him than this. Or surely this does not go wide enough or far enough or deep enough. There appear to be people, or kinds of people, whom Mr. Brooks does not fully present. Certain experiences, or certain kinds of experience, appear to be outside his sympathy or not fully within his understanding. Analyzing this impression, one comes to certain conclusions.

Mr. Brooks has an exquisite feeling for personality. Few critics have ever been able to follow so responsively the moods and quirks, the oddities and eccentricities, the individual perceptions, refractions, and reflections of writers. At recovering from a writer's work the exact personal tonality of the moment of creation he surpasses everyone else who has written criticism in America. But one grants him less mastery of character: the geography of a writer's mind, the fullness of his experience, the measure by which his work corresponds or fails to correspond to his experience. Some kinds of character and some kinds of thinking and feeling he justly transcribes. But others he deals with ineffectively and still others, I think significantly, he evades.

He is best with minor writers and with those of larger size of whom a particular kind of failure or frustration can be justly alleged. With major writers in general and with writers of whom it may be justly said that their books were shaped by personal frustration he does less well. Dr. Holmes is the best portrait of *The Flowering* — Holmes, the bright, jaunty, shallow mind, the energetic censor of manners and arbiter of elegance, the brittle, sensitive intelligence tirelessly alert, the insatiable observer and gossip, who shines so freshly still but must be seen as the happiest triumph of the second-rate in our literature.[8] And though Mr. Brooks's affection for Howells becomes in *Indian Summer* almost a love affair, the best study of that book — the best, I think, anywhere in his work — is Henry James. It is exquisite biography and exquisite criticism, it justly expresses all the values to which Mr. Brooks holds, it focuses his excellences. There are two observations to be made: that James's frustration may be seen more clearly than others as primarily a literary frustration, and that James corresponds more closely than anyone else to the image that excites Mr. Brooks's feelings, the great but defeated artist.[9]

But if frustration is adequately studied in James, it is less so in Henry Adams. There is a forthright attempt to analyze it, to show just what the failure which Adams felt consisted of. But Mr. Brooks does not penetrate to the depths where that failure originated. It was inevitable that he should decide that *Mont-Saint-Michel*, which is concerned primarily with art, is a greater book than the *Education*, which is concerned with life. It was inevitable that he should decide that Adams had "missed in his age" not the new energies which Adams knew were breaking up the world, but instead merely "the finest writers and artists that America produced." Adams's dismay, apprehension, withdrawal, and foreboding of disaster are clear to him. But he is not given to understand that they were shaped, and in large part created, by Adams's failure to be in touch with America. He does not see that the author of one great American history and one great American biography was never able to make contact with the life of his country later than their period, that the War Ambassador's secretary never understood the war, that the amateur politician, the friend of Hay and Roosevelt, was so shut off from his people that he never acquired a single trustworthy idea about them. He does not see that the frustration of Henry Adams, his abhorrence of the present, and his fear of the future all expressed his inability to enter the experience of his fellow Americans.[10]

And when it comes to a writer whose frustration was not at all literary but so intensely personal that there was no possible expression for it except great literature, the analysis breaks down altogether. What Mr. Brooks has to tell us of Emily Dickinson is a shocking trivialization of genius.[11] Something is too great for him. Clearly it is not the poetry but the ether in which the poetry exists, the neurosis. One of the foremost geniuses of our literature comes out little more than an inspired child and Mr. Brooks has fled from something too powerful to be faced.

What has he fled from, and why? One thinks back to other portraits. Longfellow — was he really so choked with honey as Mr. Brooks makes out? Did he really write those poems against slavery just to please Charles Sumner? Then why is there such passionate outrage in them? Why does that passion go unrecognized by Mr. Brooks? Was there never grief or despair behind the windows of Craigie House? Did not Longfellow's young wife die horribly? Was not the poet's sweet serenity broken by nights of anxiety about the evils of his country, by a terrible fear that war might destroy it? Was not the poet considerably more of a man? Did he not feel, hope, suffer, and despair much more intensely than he is permitted to in the exquisite colors of Mr. Brooks's prose? If it is judged that final insufficiencies crippled the talent of James Russell Lowell, why is it not considered that poverty, drudgery, and grief may have had some-

thing to do with them? His two beloved daughters died
in childhood, their mother died too, and the agony is
fierce in Lowell's poetry but it is not fierce in Mr.
Brooks's portrait.

Was there not more iron in Emerson's mind? Here
is too much care to catch "the little harlot fireflies of the
lowlands" and the firefly glimmer of Emerson's thought
along the far margin of Buddhism, but too little of the
seer's lifelong weighing of his countrymen's daily life
and the institutions that contained it, too little of his
anger, challenge, and defiance. Mr. Brooks's Emerson
lives in Concord Village and in the universe but he does
not live in the United States. The shadow which Emerson
has cast for a century, which has grown longer throughout a century, is cast primarily by the citizen — by the
native who was concerned first of all with "the meal in
the firkin, the milk in the pan," and who, if he prolonged
his thought across the universe, did so primarily that it
might serve to assess the experience of Americans. Mr.
Brooks's Emerson is a diminished man, and so is his
Thoreau. Something of nationality is gone from them,
something of completeness, and much of robustness.
They are confined too narrowly within the eidolon of
Mr. Brooks's earlier period, The Artist. They are forever threatening to degenerate into mere esthetes.

In a word, their human passions are too decorative and
too weak. One finds the passions too weak throughout
this criticism, all the passions, and all experiences too
weak except the literary ones. It is not only that in Mr.

Brooks's Whittier, for instance, the poet's hatred of slavery comes out hardly more than expository. One misses the headaches that crippled Whittier, the struggle against pain and bad health and physical weakness that made his life heroic. Surely both his struggle against evil and his struggle against weakness shaped his life and therefore his work — and therefore shaped even the mood of a poet talking to friends or sitting at his table and laboring to make words come alive, which is the mood in which Mr. Brooks chiefly sees Whittier and everyone else. We should be told something of that heat and hatred, that pain and heroism. Likewise, is it safe to dismiss from Henry Adams's life so easily as both Adams and Mr. Brooks dismiss it, the suicide of his wife? More of Henry Adams than Mr. Brooks ever touches on must, one thinks, have gone to bring about that ugly violence, and more must have issued from it as the man's thought and books ran on. And what about Parkman?

One who has worked long with Parkman is dismayed by Mr. Brooks's treatment — finding little reality in it, as if the man's character and the importance of his work had both been missed altogether. Square in any critic's path stands the edifice of Parkman's histories, the greatest achievement by an American historian. Criticism, one thinks, cannot escape the obligation of understanding it, but Mr. Brooks escapes. What Parkman's understanding of the conflict of empires on this continent was, how far it is just or unjust or eccentric or shallow or pro- found, how far we may trust our greatest historian in his report on one of our greatest experiences, or even how much it contains of men and women living and dying as the great events move across the wilderness — Mr. Brooks does not enter history by such avenues as these. Such matters lie outside the values that live for him, the composition of books. But even here, in the composition of books, a deficiency strikes one too forcibly to be ignored.

Surely the literary life was never lived more heroically than Parkman lived it, yet no adequate feeling for his agony informs Mr. Brooks's portrait. The black despair of an eyestrain that for some years withheld Parkman from work altogether and for more years limited him to five minutes a day, or one minute a day, of using his eyes, the fear of insanity, the fear of heart failure, the pain of arthritis, the insomnia, the days and nights of impotence, the fumbling with fingers along a frame of wires to guide the crayon, the fortitude of a man nobly resolved to effect his will in spite of torments of physical and mental disease — by far too little of this comes through to Mr. Brooks's page. Something had been fled from, I said of his portrait of Emily Dickinson. What was fled from there was an agony of the soul. A comparable agony and an agony of the body as well are fled from in the portrait of Parkman. An intensity, an intensity of human experience, has baffled literary criticism.

To worry the point no longer, it is just to make this finding in general about *The Flowering of New England* and *Indian Summer*. There is little intensity in them except the intensity of writers mastering a literary medium. There is little struggle in them except the struggle of writers trying to give idea a garment of words. There is little violence or even vehemence of thought, and hardly any of feeling. Is there even desire? Hardly as the experience of men and women. These writers seldom fall in love, and one feels that only those have children whose children also became writers. There is hardly pain except as literary pain, there is hardly anxiety or despair except as writers regret that their books have fallen short of their vision. I have said that they hardly live with the fellow citizens in their own country, as men to whom citizenship and the events of time and history occur. But it is also true that they live but weakly outside their studies. They hardly live as men who have been roweled by desire, who have seen love come to nothing, cursed God when a child died, lain awake at night burning in hellfire with knowledge of a son's life impaired by their stupidity, with every man's accusation of injuries inflicted on wife and friends, with the ignominy of human association bungled or betrayed. Literary ecstasy rises high for them and literary despair sinks deep, but not the ecstasy and despair of anyone's life among men.

It is not for me to inquire how far this evasion of experience may be part of the critic's temperament. It may be deeply so, or only a little, or not at all. But if temperament plays any part whatsoever in it, surely much more is attributable to the general body of ideas, assumptions, theses, and values whose anatomy I have described. There is a continuity between the work of Mr. Brooks's first period and his mature work. That continuity is an indifference to the common experience of mankind. It must have some relation to the literary fallacy.

It was an explicit theory in the first period. In the second period it is implicit — we hear nothing of it but we see it fulfilled in the critic's occupation, preoccupation, study, and practice. Seldom has there been such a sedulous winnowing of literary material. No one before him covered so completely as Mr. Brooks the books of New England writers and their biographies, autobiographies, letters, journals, memoirs, reminiscences — and those of their families and friends. It is a labor resolutely conceived and lovingly carried out. His seine has a fine mesh, it brings up not only the big fish but the smallest minnows too, together with much long forgotten, brightly colored sea stuff in which his delight is manifest. But as he works with this vast heap of variegated stuff his reference is to books, not to life — not to experience, not to society, not to the native roots or the common life or the great dream or the national tradition or any other criterion trumpeted as a challenge to writers and common folk alike when Mr. Brooks was young and indignant. The hour struck and he turned from rejecting us, from the great withdrawal, to make the great affirmation. But, as before, he appealed to books and not to the life from which books come.

How should it be otherwise? Too deep in him ever to be questioned was the belief that books are the apex of the cultural hierarchy, that literature holds culture in solution. Writers — The Artist — are the end toward which a civilization moves, from writers a civilization can be recovered and known and felt, and by writers it shall be judged. A culture is to be appraised by the criteria of literary values. So that literature becomes the goal of culture, so that literature comes to equate with life, so that literature comes to be greater than life.

But that is only another statement of the literary fallacy. One who accepts it can make, I think, only superficial objections to what American literary criticism has to say in, as one example, Mr. Brooks's mature work. But one who cannot accept it must say that, rewarding as that work unquestionably is, it is nevertheless only a history of books. It is criticism of books, out of books, by the sole means of books, to the sole end of books. It is neither history nor criticism of literature if literature is an artery flowing the bloodstream of men or nations. It is neither history nor criticism of literature if literature has an organic bond with experience. It is neither history nor criticism of literature unless literature is coextensive with culture.

This, then, is the utmost that the strain of literary thinking we deal with can accomplish. At its warmest, at its most brilliant, it ends in, to use one of its favorite terms, frustration. Critics who have held more rigorously than Mr. Brooks to the original theses have not fared otherwise. If we had time it would be instructive to examine literary thinking at its extremity, in the crystal palace of Mr. T. S. Eliot. Mr. Eliot has many distinctions, among them that of having written the poem in which this entire movement agreed to find its age expressed. He conceived himself to belong to such an Academy as the young Brooks had envisaged, a supreme court of writers which would appraise the worth of experience (it has seemed to have room for only one bench), and a legislature of writers to whose decrees society would best conform. No one else who has written English in our time has spoken with such a high consciousness of a writer's authority — or with such contempt of extra-literary experience. No one else who has written criticism in English at any time has so straitly narrowed it to an assessment of literary experience conceived solely as abstract idea. But Mr. Eliot escapes altogether from such an examination as this. We cannot say that in his work criticism has been divorced from life, for the marriage oath was never taken. The intent was always to devote it to a single aspect of literary idea, the epistemological aspect. Mr. Eliot withdrew from experience not by fallacy but by voluntary act. He would erect a structure of pure thought, not in a humble expectation that any who came after him might convert it to human use, but in a determination that any use found for it by any except writers would, for writers, make it uninhabitable.

To examine the final frustration of criticism we should have to explore in detail the decade that followed the one in which I have been seeking its roots, and that would require another course of lectures. When the disasters of our era began to reveal their shape in the 1930's, many critics were indeed shaken out of their purely literary preoccupations. The vow then taken (or rather repeated, for how does it differ from Mr. Brooks's manifesto of 1915?) that literature shall be held to the expression of life might eventually break the frustration. But the curve of the arc is still downward. It is not my finding but that of criticism itself that in its new occupations also it still finds frustration, that in fact it is not merely frustrated but ignominiously routed. When critics undertook to face the collapse of the world order, they once more asserted the necessity of literature to deal directly with society, to purify or reform it, and even to make it over by revolution. They eagerly picked up tools which criticism had lately disdained, tools shaped by the physical and biological sciences and the social sciences. But it proved that the new tools would work for them only to the old ends, and usually with less responsibility. The perils of society were too complex, they were too terrifying, and the comfort of abstractions and cliques was too easily invoked. For some the Marxian hypotheses supplied the certainty that had lately been drawn from esthetic axioms. Like esthetic axioms they proved capable of repudiating our society altogether while at the same time they excused writers of any responsibility of honesty or knowledge, and relieved them of any action beyond that of watching a mechanical determinism fulfill itself. Other literary ideas in other hands proved just as powerless to reconstruct society.

One coterie failed as their predecessors had failed, in that the speeches of John C. Calhoun were no more effective against industrialism in 1935 than they had been in 1860, or than Turgenev's notebooks had been in 1915, or indeed the doctrines of Charles Fourier had been in 1846 when, in almost the same terms, the Brook Farmers came to the same end.

Still others have distilled the literary fallacy to an even purer essence. They have reached a point where they prefer to talk not even about books as a substitute for experience but rather about parts of books, sometimes parts so fragmented from the rest that they seem no more than the syntax of a single page. From such fragmentation it was a short step to semantics. Not what a writer might say about life interested them now but only the meaning of his words as words, alphabetical symbols capable of being assigned algebraic values. And lately they have preferred to take these symbols not from imaginative literature — not from writers who at least try to deal directly with life — but from one another. Thus literary criticism, which began by abstaining from life, has come to abstain even from literature. It has become what a gusty phrase of Mencken's once called it, the criticism of the criticism of criticism. Criticism has restored a dignity long denied to the rhetorician's trade, and to anyone who might reproach it for regarding neither life nor literature, the present postulates would reply that, till agreement on terms can be reached, there is no reason why it should. It began by undertaking to reconstruct society. It ends by sternly requiring an opponent to be sure that he is using technical terms correctly.

This, bear in mind, is what systematic criticism is now saying about itself. Twenty-five years ago it set out to explain what it held to be the sterility of American culture. Now it confesses itself culturally sterile, and there is something winsome in Mr. Kazin's recent wonder how it got that way. The answer is simple. If literary criticism has achieved paralysis, it got there by following strictly literary paths, by applying its own conceptions in accordance with its own methods. If it ends self-supported in pure air, unattached to American experience or any other experience, that end followed inevitably from the beginning. The effort to appraise a culture by means of purely literary criteria had no possible outcome except failure.

Notes

1. ". . . although many years passed before he read Howells's novels. He was forty-five before he knew how good they were." (*Allston*, p. 22) "As all we Americans did, I conducted my education in public. . . ." (*Ibid.*, p. 27)

2. This is charmingly shown by the last chapter of Alfred Kazin's *On Native Grounds*, the best study of modern American literature so far written. Mr. Kazin has a much wider critical base than any of his predecessors, a much richer knowledge of the nonliterary content of our culture, and a tolerant and flexible understanding. But one reads that last chapter, for instance, with an uneasy suspicion. Thus, he apparently believes that in the 1940's, and specifically with such books as Carl Van Doren's *Benjamin Franklin* and Carl Sandburg's *Abraham Lincoln*, honest, deep-seeking, objective, and informed biographies were written for the first time in America. He is as indifferent as the earlier Brooks to a century of American history and biography — or as ignorant of it. Or again, what he says about the WPA guidebooks naïvely assumes that their effort to report the color and diversity of local scenes and humble people was something altogether new to our literature. (And something very useful to Mr. Kazin's emerging thesis.) The guidebooks are a magnificent achievement, one which I have no desire to disparage. But Mr. Kazin ought, before he said a word about them, to have learned that as guides they followed models long before set up by the Geological Survey and that as history they were almost altogether compendiums. They utilize not only the vast monographic literature of professional historians, which Mr. Kazin leaves out of account, but the vaster literature of antiquarians and local historical societies, which is destructive of Mr. Kazin's thesis. This amateur history — the loving, conscientious,

tireless, frequently absurd work of altogether unpresumptu-
ous enthusiasts — has been a rich part of our cultural heritage
since long before the beginning of the Republic. It would
have been absurd of the WPA editors not to use it. It is
absurd of Mr. Kazin not to know that they did — he lapses
into the literary fallacy.

3. "The Anti-Slavery Writers" and "The Younger Generation of 1870."

4. He studies the opposition to slavery purely in the
books written about it, which, even by strict literary values,
is a mistake of the first magnitude. He actually says that
John Woolman, a writer, began the anti-slavery movement,
and repeats as literally true Lincoln's amiable greeting to
Mrs. Stowe, that she caused the Civil War. His discussion
of *Uncle Tom's Cabin* involves historical findings that belong to fantasy.

5. Poets and novelists of our time have not, God knows,
been unaware of the Civil War, but most critical systems
have exhibited an unawareness similar to Mr. Brooks's and
probably to be explained on the same grounds. It is true that
the "agrarian" critics have dealt with it; one might say that
they have dealt with little else. It is also true that the proletarian critics had a neat cliché about it, derived from their
holy book; the trouble was that, though the cliché neatly
explained the war, it proved to be in embarrassing conflict
with other scriptural theses. Most critics, however, either
ignored the Civil War or added it to the Literary Credo —
it was to be thought of as something that produced the
Gilded Age. The inviolable introspection of the literary
view shows clearly when one remembers that precisely at
this same time American historians were studying the Civil
War as a fundamental experience of the American people,
as perhaps the most important single part of our past. His-

torians, that is, were actually making the reappraisal which the systematic thinkers set out to make.

6. He condemns Bancroft as a political opportunist, understanding that Bancroft joined the Democratic Party because advancement in the Whig Party was closed to him. A just understanding of our past — and of our present — requires one to understand the recurrent, sometimes violent expansions of popular political control. It would seem impossible to understand this marked continuity without understanding the movement loosely called Jacksonian Democracy. Mr. Brooks shows little awareness either of Jacksonism or of the current it belonged to, which is why he does Bancroft an injustice. Bancroft was one of the intellectuals who composed Jackson's brain trust. He was a working partner of such men as Francis Blair, Amos Kendall, and others who formulated the social and political philosophy of the movement. He played an honorable part in shaping some of our conceptions of democracy.

7. Even *Two Years before the Mast* is called a poem about the beauty of ships.

8. The portrait is masterly and must affect the reputation of Holmes from now on. Nevertheless, and in spite of the fact that Holmes is certainly not underpraised, one aspect of his mind is done something less than justice. Mr. Brooks treats Holmes's scientific thinking chiefly in relation to *Elsie Venner*, undervalues his prescience and heroic obstinacy about puerperal fever, neglects the content of his Medical School lectures, and in general writes down a phase of Holmes which the future is likely to write up. The Holmes who was tirelessly interested in all the unfolding science of his day, who eagerly investigated and theorized about photography as soon as it was introduced in America, the Holmes of the stereoscope and endless other novelties,

the Holmes of the *New England Journal of Medicine* —
here is a man as yet insufficiently appreciated, whose curiosity and vitality did much for our cultural heritage that
did not get expressed in his verse and essays.

9. That image appears and reappears throughout his
work — in the preconceptions of the earlier books, in the
soliloquies of *Oliver Allston,* in his many studies of failure
and his praise of those who praise it. I note how often in
his mature work Mr. Brooks turns from the goals usually
considered proper to criticism in order to make minute
registrations of consciousness which are usually considered
proper to fiction. Does he identify himself with the image
of the defeated artist?

10. One of many excellences of Mr. Charles Beard's introduction to a recent reprint of *The Law of Civilization
and Decay* is that it clearly shows intimate relations between
Henry Adams's ideas and those of his brother Brooks.
Further study, I think, will go even farther. It appears to
me that Brooks was the original thinker and Henry the
great stylist. Brooks seems to have originated not only the
analysis of the financial upheavals of the 1890's which
merged with Henry's talks with Langley and study of Gibbs
to produce laws of history, he seems to have originated also
the concepts of physical force which Henry brought to the
study of those laws.

Mr. Brooks sees that there was a relationship between
Henry's ideas about America and his brother Charles's business career but does not analyze it. An analysis of that
relationship is badly needed, and it might well begin by
analyzing that business career. In fact, a great deal of spadework on the Adamses remains to be done. Why has no one
since Charles Francis, Jr., discussed the family in relation to
the family belief that American history was something
which occurred inside the ties of blood?

The theme of *The Education of Henry Adams* is the failure of its author to make effective contact with his age in America. Though the theme is sounded on the first page criticism has not yet studied it in detail. Criticism has freely conceded that Adams knew little about any people except his few intimates, most of them politicians, almost all of them narrowly caste-conscious, but it has never investigated how that fact may have distorted his conceptions. Even on the level of national politics, where he believed himself an adept and an initiate, his letters show him more often wrong than right about what was happening within his hearing and before his eyes. How life was lived in America and what kind of people lived it outside the Back Bay, Washington, and the state government of Pennsylvania (which, as the corrupt Cameron machine governed it, Henry actually held to be the best adaptation made by American democracy), were wholly unimportant to him. The South is a personal symbol to him down to 1865; after that it ceases even to be a symbol. The West hardly exists except as a place which Clarence King is inexplicably interested in. One will make note of unkempt demagogues who invade the society of the genteel from both sections, but one will not bother to wonder why they come. An unacknowledged novel will record the distress they can inflict on the master caste; one's memoirs will record their triumph over that class — and, like Spengler, convert the episode into a philosophy of history. But the way to understand them is to be sought in the mathematics of solar energy.

11. Even Mr. Whicher's book, the only good one yet written about Emily Dickinson, does not seriously face the neurosis which is one of the most striking in literary history and is certainly the master condition of her poetry. Mr. Brooks meets Emily's father squarely in his path but he makes nothing of that image in her poetry, or of her

brother who became its surrogate. Her two recurring themes are God and love. The God of whom she speaks with such a jocularly reverent accusation that He has betrayed her by being less than God must somehow equate with her father. The love whose fire is phosphorescent and without heat is forbidden by unalterable law, and clearly relates more to her brother's love affair than to her own. Yet when the criticism of the 1920's approached her with instruments which it understood to be Freudian, it usually found that, like Melville, she had been defeated by industrial Puritanism.

IV

Waste Land

M R. LEWIS GANNETT once alluded to "the hurt boy" who must be held responsible for much of Sinclair Lewis's work. Mr. Malcolm Cowley has studied the image of the young man so much more sensitive than the rude folk around him who appears so often in the fiction of the 1920's. A leading novelist of that decade, as an amusing conceit, itemized a collection of books which great writers of the past ought for our sake to have written but neglected to write. These are useful ideas but they provoke irreverence or even ribaldry. I have sometimes aspired to write a literary history of the 1920's describing the books which the decade might have produced *if*. If the lines had fallen to certain writers otherwise than they did.

What shapes might the literature of the 1920's have taken? If, instead of being reared in a nostalgia of the Stephen A. Douglas tradition, Mr. Edgar Lee Masters had been enlisted as a comer by the Republican politicians of Spoon River? If F. Scott Fitzgerald, instead of breaking a leg in a dolorous October, had been able to play on the freshman football team at Princeton? If Mr. Floyd Dell had been more adept at making small talk for the high school girls of Davenport? If a more critical public opinion had restrained Harold Stearns from writing book reviews and reconstructing society until such time as his ideas had grown adult enough to shave? If the talents of Mr. Ben Hecht had found their way not to the *Chicago Daily News* but to Batten, Barton, Durstine & Osborn? If the generic novelist of the period had first experienced sin in a hayloft instead of the books of Havelock Ellis, had grown up with more children of the village atheist and fewer members of the Epworth League, or had studied English at high school under the basketball coach instead of the generic middle-aged woman who admired the poems of Thomas Bailey Aldrich in the *Atlantic Monthly?*

Such speculations pollute the dignity of criticism, however, and it will be best to use another approach.

It would be illiberal to refuse such critics as I have been dealing with classification as imaginative writers but we must in some degree distinguish between literary thinkers and literary artists. Artists tend to lack skill at formal logic. They lack the staying power of systematic thinkers and tend to lapse from the strict construction of theses. Furthermore, their inner compulsions are more egoistic and the nature of their media requires even the most docile of them to try to work directly with experience instead of making the abstractions from it which give critical ideas their symmetry. In any period it is the critics who work out general ideas; artists tend rather to apply them in detail than as a system. They tend to apply the end products, too, rather than the initial assumptions. We should not expect the novelists or the poets of the 1920's to conform always to the dominant critical system nor to work altogether within the literary fallacy. Nevertheless, on the whole they certainly did take instruction from the system. Between them and the material they set out to work with the literary fallacy did indeed stretch a membrane of theory, assumption, or prepossession which impaired their function. It is rather an attitude or a state of mind than the application of logical instruments, and what we find is infection or radiation rather than systematic investigation or report. I cannot take you through the literature of a decade in one lecture. I propose merely to examine the evidence of certain illustrations which seem to me to exhibit a relationship and a rough kind of harmony. They are all from the main current of the decade's literature, the official literature, the literature praised by writers themselves. They are also, whether consciously or unconsciously, within the final limitations imposed by the literary fallacy.

Sinclair Lewis will be remembered as the author of four novels, *Main Street, Babbitt, Arrowsmith,* and *Elmer Gantry.* Our purpose would permit us to approach them in a number of ways. We might say that their rationale shows a progressive shift from the ideas of Mr. Van Wyck Brooks to those of Mr. H. L. Mencken. We might say that their description of America is considerably more sociological than anything we have previously considered. We might say that although they show an energetic repudiation of American experience it is not an irreconcilable repudiation or even a fundamental one. We certainly ought to say that they have a greater gusto than any other fiction of the period. They are first-rate novels, and Mr. Lewis may well be the best novelist of the decade. But I have time only to inquire whether something which they lack may not be a common, and significant, lack in the literature of the period as a whole. I propose merely to inquire what Mr. Lewis's novels praise.

The critics have never been sure whether Mr. Lewis was trying to truly represent the life of his time or to caricature it, and it seems likely that Mr. Lewis has shared their uncertainty. Satire, however, has an important prerogative. So long as we understand what a satirist is driving at, we cannot ask him to tell the whole truth about it. The faithful representation of reality which other kinds of novelists hold to be their highest duty lays no obligation on him. But also there is a touchstone to satire: it has points of reference which make its values clear. Thus the spirited portraiture in *Main Street* withholds you from asking whether some aspects of life in Gopher Prairie may not have been distorted or ignored until you wonder what the town is being held against for reference. You discover that the reference is to certain adolescent ideas of Carol Kennicott. And suddenly it appears that the Village Virus which has poisoned America consists of the failure of small towns to support productions of the one-act plays of Eugene O'Neill, to provide candlelight at dinner, and to sanction lounging pajamas as evening wear for housewives. The superb evocation of the city of Zenith in *Babbitt* distracts one from values until one comes to consider the side of George F. Babbitt with whom Mr. Lewis finally developed a warm friendship and to consider the few inhabitants of the city who are held to be living the good life. Whereupon there appears so trivial an imagination of deep experience, so shallow and unsophisticated a conception of emotional relationships and intellectual activity, that one sees at once what has been left out of Zenith. What has been left out is human profundity, whether admirable or base.

Finally, when a novelist creates heroes he comes out into the open. Mr. Lewis's understanding is illuminated for us by *Arrowsmith*. Here he not only undertakes to make a sociologist's survey of the entire field of medicine in America; he also undertakes to exalt the scientific ideal and to praise a way of life which he thinks of as heroic. We may dismiss the survey as within the prerogatives of satire, though Mr. Lewis's virtuosity blinds one to the ferocious injustice done to the Public Health Service, institutions like the Rockefeller Foundation, medical research in general, and the customary life of doctors. It is not that Mr. Lewis's Jacques Loeb, Professor Gottlieb, is contained altogether in a solution of romantic tears, or that his Metchnikoff, Dr. Sondelius, is a sophomore scientist seen sophomorically. It is rather that these characters show his conception of scientific inquiry to be debased. And in Martin Arrowsmith, the details of his career, his mind and thinking and emotions, his science and the larger science it is bound to, are romantic, sentimental, and above all trivial. Himself an adolescent whose experience is never mature or complex, he is portrayed in an adolescent conception of what he stands for. As a mind Martin suffers from arrested development, as a scientist he is a fool. Mr. Lewis does indeed picture certain genuine absurdities of scientific research in the book, but never the really dangerous absurdities. And the austerity, complexity, illuminations, frustrations, methods, goals, and conditions of scientific thinking never get into the book at all. The realities of science, worthy or unworthy, the great world of science in its entirety, are altogether passed by.

Is not the same true of Mr. Lewis's characters in general? Leora Arrowsmith is emotionally undeveloped. Ann Vickers is an immature mind and her emotions are childlike. Dodsworth is so simple a personality that one doubts if he could have managed a corporation. His wife Fran, who is Lewis's most developed character, is not developed past a simple statement of frigidity, a statement which does not disclose either the content or the roots of frigidity. Maturity of mind, maturity of emotion, complexity of character or experience, profundity of aspiration, despair, achievement, or failure — they are not discoverable in these books. They are not present in America so far as these books try to be an index to America. Mr. Lewis is not at ease when he is on the side of his characters, he is at ease when he is deriding them, when they are his butts. But his attack on them consists of showing that they are without complexity, sophistication, true power, or genuine depth. Select whatever you will, love, lust, family affection, courage, meditation, fantasy, childhood, religion, socialism, education, friendship, villainy, pain — and you find it shallow. The lives explored are uncomplicated, the experience revealed is mediocre.

Again there is no point in asking whether some part of this may be a defect of the novelist, for even if any be, a greater part certainly originates in the literary fallacy. In Mr. Lewis's work a sizable portion of our literature went out to answer questions whose answers it had worked out as assumptions in advance. The rationale existed beforehand as a chart, and when literature inquired what American life was like, it knew in advance that American life would turn out to be trivial, shallow, and mediocre. It is a short step from mediocrity to contemptibility. In the mood to which Mr. Lewis brought more energy, talent, enjoyment, and even affection than anyone else, novelists for a long time conceived of fiction as an exercise in expressing the contemptibility of American life. True to the pattern of fads, fiction began to develop specific types. There was the farm novel: frustra-

tion, cretinism, bastardy, and the squalor of the soul.
A current folkway of writers was to seek the good life
on little farms in Connecticut, whence frustrate peasants
had been driven out, but the novel of farm life as un-
speakably degraded moved all across our geography till
the Pacific Ocean put a boundary to it. There was the
novel of Prohibition, the novel of the repressed high
school teacher, the novel of the American male as an
unskilled lover, the novel which daringly denounced the
courthouse gang — but a more studious mind than I has
made a list. An admirer of this fiction, which he called
the novel of protest, once set out to name its principal
themes, with no apparent knowledge that he was writing
humor: —

the American passion for "bigness" and success, high
pressure salesmanship, shoddy commercial products,
poor housing conditions in urban areas, the narrow,
lethargic, platitudinous, and often hysterical mob
mind, corruption in government, labor injunctions,
racketeering, standardization in education, industry,
and art, the deportation of radicals, the abridgment
of our constitutional liberties, the contract system of
prison labor, militarism, the subsidizing of large
corporations, political patronage, blue laws, nation-
alism, the legalized extortion of big business, sweat
shops in the needle trades, racial prejudice, the
stretch system in factories, inelastic marriage stat-
utes, capital punishment, the entrance of religion

into politics, imperialism, profiteering, a nation half boom and half broke, jingoism, rate inflation by public utilities, law evasions, our present jury system, election frauds, bigotry, child labor, the Ku Klux Klan, and wage slavery of every kind.

Of this sort of thing criticism has lately been saying that fiction had turned from experience to data, and that is true. But such a list merely names some of the ways in which fiction was finding the Americans mediocre or contemptible. One observes an omission: the list makes no finding that literary persons are mediocre or may be considered contemptible. However, in due time Mr. Hemingway was to close that gap.

By process of critical rationale, by dedication, by fashion, by a variety of other avenues, writers have come to occupy the site chosen for them by Mr. Brooks, for which Mr. Cabell found a suggestive name, the High Place. Biography has become a study of mediocrity and contemptibility in our past, apparently to excuse us by accusing our ancestors. Like fiction and criticism, it is a withdrawal to the High Place. Some writers, following Harold Stearns's manifesto, are making a literal withdrawal. In American society there is no joy nor light nor hope, no dignity, no worth; reality cannot be found there and art cannot live. So the Artist will seek societies where art can live, finding joy and hope and beauty, experience deep in the grain, Paris, the French Riviera, Cornwall, the Mediterranean islands, Russia. What life in America abundantly lacks exists abundantly in such places. Thought is free there, art is the universal goal of human effort, writers are universally respected, and human life has a claim on the interest of literary men which in America it assuredly has not. But whether physical or only spiritual, the withdrawal to the High Place has become an established mode of literature and this mode dominates the literature to which the generality of writers acknowledge allegiance. The dedication of the High Place may be granted easily, but the illumination of its inhabitants seems to consist of perceiving the inferiorities of their countrymen. Few writers ever spoke of themselves in print as a superior class. The assumption is implicit in the critical rationale, but it is customary to speak not of superiority but of leadership. The superiority of the caste is the inferiority of the life withdrawn from. From the High Place, the Americans are the fall guys of the world, sometimes dangerous as a mob, less often pitiful as well-meaning boobs, but most often tawdry, yokelish, acquisitive, coarse, an undifferentiated mass preyed on by mass passions and dominated by mass fears.

Turn now to Mr. Ernest Hemingway's fiction for evidence to carry us a little farther. Here are memorable portraits of racketeers, thugs, hunters of big and small game, prizefighters, bullfighters, poolroom hangers-on, prostitutes, expatriate idlers, soldiers, a miscellany of touts, sportsmen, entertainers and the like, and some millionaires and writers of whom the principal assertion

is that they are sexually impotent. Mr. Hemingway's
themes are death, the fear of death, the defiance of death,
and the dangers to which male potency is exposed — and
it is easy to see what he praises. He praises aggressiveness,
courage, male wariness, male belligerence, the instinctual
life, war and fighting, sexual intercourse, and a few primary loyalties immediately associated with them. It is
also easy to say what life is not, as his fiction represents
life. Life, so far as it can be desired or respected, does not
exist above the diaphragm. It is activated by digestion,
the surge of adrenalin into the bloodstream at crises of
danger or defiance, and the secretion of the testicles. His
hero is a pre-Piltdown stage of man, a warily aggressive
anthropoid who goes down fighting. Intellectual life does
not exist even in rudimentary form, except that the contempt heaped on it grants it a kind of existence. There is
no social life, there is not even a society. Pithecanthropus
Erectus prowls a swamp so sown with danger that the
honors, constraints, bonds, prohibitions, and decencies
of men living together merely add another, extreme form
of danger to it. They are weaknesses of less perfect
animalities who have risen to the ethical and social development of, say, Cro-Magnon man; the superior, more
primitive anthropoid merely uses them to destroy him.
There is hardly even love, though Mr. Hemingway has
written many love stories, one of which may well be the
best of his period. Piltdown man couples with his female
and the physical mating is clean, but the beauty of this
function is corrupted when love tries to add spiritual

associations to it. They are decadent — anything is decadent which may diminish male vigor or deflect its functioning. Life has grandeur in that it may aggressively defy violent death, and it has tragedy in that the defiance may be vain.

In short, the world most of us live in and the qualities by which we try to live are unrecognized in Mr. Hemingway's fiction. True, criticism has decided that the progress of world disorder finally led him to a great affirmation, and Mr. Geismar, whom I have quoted before, seems honestly to believe that the doom of civilization was averted and hope came back to the Western world when Mr. Hemingway found a cause he could believe in. Still, it does not appear that the dying murderer of *To Have and Have Not* has altered Mr. Hemingway's basic values when he has learned that adrenalin spurts in vain into the bloodstream of one man alone. Nor, after prayerful search, can I find that the values by which the life of men is to be judged have been altered in the novel to which Mr. Hemingway so presumptuously prefixed a quotation from John Donne. It is true that Mr. Hemingway's constant preoccupation with belligerence, cruelty, and inflicted death has contrived to associate itself with symbols in which the rest of us find values that ennoble life. But in the novel life is not ennobled by those symbols. The emphasis still suggests that though the sexual act may be very fine, the act of killing is an orgasm far surpassing it in intensity. The world for which Robert Jordan faithfully sacrifices his life appears to be, in prospect, still a swamp which men who are mere bowels and autonomic nervous systems will prowl to the same ends, though perhaps this time in bands of gangsters rather than as lonely killers. The novel is not aware, even in vision, of society as civilization or of life as something affected by the fore-brain.

From the beginning up to now, both implicitly and explicitly, with a vindictive belligerence, Mr. Hemingway has always attacked the life of the mind, the life of the spirit, and the shared social experience of mankind. Certainly he finds them contemptible; it is a legitimate guess that they scare him. The point is, however, that his disdain of intelligence, contempt of spirituality, praise of mindlessness, and adoration of instinct and blood-consciousness have many connections with other literary values held elsewhere in the general movement. They are related to the cult of pure esthetics, to the mystical cult of which D. H. Lawrence was the most gifted exponent in English, to the manias of doom that obsess Mr. Falkner (who has much else in common with Mr. Hemingway), and to such clotted phobias as those that distinguish the work of Robinson Jeffers. If some areas of literature made a thesis of the inferiority of Americans, other areas exalted the thesis to make men inferior to the animals. It is a short step from thinking of the mob to thinking of the wolf pack, from the praise of instinct to war against reason, from art's vision of man as contemptible to dictatorship's vision of men as slaves. Such considerations, however, do not concern us. We have

merely to repeat that Mr. Hemingway's fiction is separated from our common experience. By a different path
he has come to the High Place. He is uncomfortable
there for he finally comes to use the word "writer" as
an epithet of contempt, as folklore has the wounded
snake striking its fangs into its own body. But there he
is and love, work, decency, achievement, aspiration, and
defeat, as people know them who are neither writers nor
bullfighters nor anthropoids, do not come within his
awareness. Or, if they sometimes intrude on him, they
only press the trigger of his scorn.

I think that we have enough clues now and may let
the rest of the period's literature go undescribed, coming
forthwith to the symbols which this literature agreed to
accept as comprehending the whole. What this generation had to say about life, it was generally agreed, found
final expression in Mr. Eliot's poem, "The Waste Land."
I do not propose to add to the thousands of pages that
have analyzed it, but only to mention the passage in
which Tiresias, "Old man with wrinkled female breasts,"
is present at the tawdry seduction of the typist home at
teatime by the young man carbuncular, the small house
agent's clerk on whom assurance sits as a silk hat on a
Bradford millionaire. Here thirty concentrated lines of
verse render life in the modern world as a cheap inanity,
love as a vulgar ritual without feeling or significance, and
mankind as too unimportant to justify Mr. Eliot's hatred
of Apeneck Sweeney.

It is a crucial passage, crucial not only in Mr. Eliot's
poetry but in the literature of our time. All Mr. Eliot's

other perceptions support it, down to the time when his
forehead was crossed with ashes on the first day of a later
Lent. In it an entire literary movement makes a final
judgment. Literature looks at human beings and says that
this is what their experience amounts to. It commits itself. Then, having made the commitment, Mr. Eliot went
on to prophesy. He was right to do so. For if personality
and experience in our time were justly rendered in this
passage, then there could be little doubt that life must
come out as he predicted.

> This is the way the world ends
> This is the way the world ends
> This is the way the world ends
> Not with a bang but a whimper.

It happens that Mr. MacLeish had a moment of shar-
ing this vision, and he envisaged the end of the world
coming down upon a gaudy circus performance when
"The armless ambidextrian was lighting A match between his great and second toe," and then above the
white faces and dazed eyes of the audience

> There in the sudden blackness the black pall
> Of nothing, nothing, nothing — nothing at all.

Literature, I say, had committed itself. It had made a
final judgment. It had reached the end of a road. In
homelier words, it had got out on the end of a limb. So
then the end of the world arrived.

Who are the people to whom Mr. MacLeish has been

appealing so passionately — on behalf of whom he has accused writers of being as irresponsible as common criminals? They are only that audience of white faces and dazed eyes whom even judgment day could not stir to an awareness of anything at all. And when the end of the world came no whimpering was to be heard, except perhaps a literary whimpering, but the typist home at teatime and young man carbuncular decided that the world should not end. Nothing whatever changed in the typist and the house agent's clerk when the bombers came over London or the shock of Pearl Harbor traveled across this country. But war provided an appeal of judgment. The typist and the clerk had fortitude, sacrifice, fellowship; they were willing to die as an act of faith for the preservation of hope. They were hope, the soul and body of hope. They were staunchness, resolution, dedication. In fact they were incommensurable with what Mr. Eliot's poem had said they were. In "The Waste Land," I remarked, an entire literary movement made a final judgment on mankind. It committed itself. It got out on the end of a limb. But mankind turned out to be otherwise. It was not what literature had said it was. Furthermore, literature is now, temporarily at least, willing to accept the reversal of judgment. It has, temporarily at least, agreed to accept courage, fortitude, sacrifice, dedication, fellowship, willingness to die for the sake of the future — it has agreed to accept such attributes as a norm by which mankind shall be judged.

But perhaps it was the business of literature all along

to take account of such attributes. It was not the typist and the young man carbuncular who were trivial. It was not their experience nor their emotions nor the realities they lived by that were trivial. It was the imagination of writers who passed judgment on them.

Return to the question I asked toward the beginning of these lectures. If one who was ignorant of American life during the 1920's, say Mr. Geismar, were to consult the books of, say, Mencken, Lewis, Hemingway, Dos Passos, and Wolfe in an effort to understand it, could he trust their description? I answered no. We have come far enough to turn that answer into an inquiry.

Consider the work of Mr. Dos Passos. No insincerity can be alleged against him, no malice, no kind of irresponsibility, especially the kind which Mr. MacLeish charges against the generation. Mr. Dos Passos has an austere conception of the responsibility of a novelist. All his fiction proceeds from a vision of life in America since the turn of the twentieth century, a vision of the time and the society as a whole. It is conceived with great power. It is worked out with a technical mastery which no contemporary has excelled. It is never suffered to depart from his vision.

One might, of course, hold that this vision is sometimes mistaken. Thus the damage done to our society by his Ward Moorehouses and Charley Andersons would indeed have been insignificant if such men had been what they seem to Mr. Dos Passos — if they had been just feeble timeservers or drunken lechers, antlike creatures carried crazily on chips by a great flood. But they were able to damage our society because that is precisely what they were not. Because Ward Moorehouse had a powerful intelligence which he employed in clearly calculated operations with effectively mastered tools. Because Charley Anderson, as a class, did not spend his time in debauchery but instead with an ascetic sobriety and an undeviating single-mindedness operated a mastered technology in his own service, toward ends which he did not in the least misconceive.

Specific inaccuracies, however, are less important for our study than the enveloping conditions in which Mr. Dos Passos's characters exist. They are always held to his vision with complete fidelity. But, ferocious as the injuries inflicted on them are, they do not move us much. These half-drugged men and women marching past milestones of indignity toward graceless deaths do not engage us to share their pain. The truth is that they hardly seem to suffer pain. Nothing theoretical or ideological is missing. Art has not failed to put any of its instruments at the service of life. Nevertheless these creatures, these integrations of behavior, are removed so far from us that they seem to be seen through a reducing glass. They lack a vital quality, they seem like automatons. It is as if, shall I say, the doom they meet is merely a literary doom.

If one sets against them the characters of the most considerable American novelist developed during the 1930's, James Farrell, one sees at once what the vital lack is. Mr. Dos Passos and Mr. Farrell conceive the function

of fiction identically. But when a Farrell character is in-
jured he bleeds, and when society wrongs one the reader
is wronged with him, and this fails to happen in the Dos
Passos novels. Certainly Mr. Dos Passos does not lack
anger or compassion — nor the irony and pity which Mr.
Hemingway found so funny when a bigger man than he
praised them. But he remains on the High Place when
looking at his people. His vision is afar off, from the
mountain top. Whereas the monstrous cruelties inflicted
on Studs Lonigan and the O'Neills, the monstrous bru-
talities they are forced to commit, are indeed monstrous
precisely because they are not seen from the mountain
top. They are monstrous because we feel that they are
an intolerable impairment of human dignity. Precisely
because human life is thought of as having inherent
worth, things done to men may indeed be intolerable.
Precisely because the experience of men has dignity there
may be tragic experience. Precisely because men are not
contemptible the cruelty and injustice inflicted on them
can move us to say this must not be borne.

With Mr. Farrell for illustration, however, I have
come outside the decade. It is proper to consider some
who in that decade stood outside the official doctrines
and made the affirmation I have found in him. But first
let me a little generalize what we have said so far.

We have examined a system of ideas which held that
American culture was barren and American life mal-
formed, tawdry, and venal. From this the next step, soon
taken, was to find the cultural traditions actively evil

and the life they expressed vile. It is easy to say that from
this literature was gone a sense of the heroic in our past.
It is easy to say that American literature had lost all feeling of the greatness of America, whether past or present,
and of its place in the Western world and its promise to
civilization. It is easy to say that belief in the future, the
very feeling of hope, was gone. But to say this is superficial, for much more was gone.

Not only heroes are scarce in this literature. In books
which leading writers wrote and leading critics praised,
the gospel of the established church, nothing is so rare
as merely decent people. Where in the literature of the
1920's is the man or woman who lived a civilized life
dedicated to the mature values of civilization? Where
is the man who accepts the ordinary decencies and prac-
tises them with good will, meeting with self-respect and
courage the human adventure of birth, growth, education, love, parenthood, work, and death? The man who
is loyal to his friends, believes in his country, is a good
citizen, loves his wife, works for his family, brings up
his children, and deals resolutely with the vicissitudes,
strains, anxieties, failures, and partial successes that com-
pose our common lot? In the official Scriptures that man
either does not exist at all or exists as an object of derision. Mr. Dos Passos overlooks him, he is beyond the
concern of Mr. Falkner, Mr. Hemingway says that he
lacks maleness, and when Mr. Lewis abandons his amiable or occasionally dangerous fools he is unable to conceive that man above the level of a high school boy.

Here criticism usually demurs. The final phase of finance capitalism, the cynicism of an inflationary boom, Prohibition, racketeering, the decay of politics, the Scopes trial, the Sacco-Vanzetti case, innumerable other data of the same kind — such evidence as this, we are told, appalled writers, who were right to dissociate themselves from it altogether. With an odd pride Mr. Edmund Wilson has remarked that this generation of writers attacked their culture more unanimously and more continuously than any other known to history. Even so, a vagrant mind wonders why orthodox dogma was unable to perceive in America any will to oppose these things except among literary folk. One goes on to point out, moreover, that not only decency and right-eousness are gone from the people whom this literature exploits but, as well, the simple basis of humanity. And that, one decides, makes merely silly the distress which criticism tells us was behind the exploitation. If man is a predatory animal, then surely it is silly of writers to blame him when he acts according to his nature. The wolf may not be hated for wolfishness nor the boob for stupidity: the anger of literature would be idiotic. But the idea that writers might be idiotic is abhorrent and so, summing up, one turns from it to say instead that literature's dissociation from common experience, achieved by systematic logic, results in a fundamental judgment, and a false judgment, on the nature of man.

Permit me a digression. For some months a job that I had been assigned required me to listen to propaganda broadcasts beamed at the United States from the fascist powers. Every so often I heard a voice well known to me through a good many years, chanting in a curious parody of solemn high mass hundreds of judgments about this country and its people which the years had made even more familiar than the voice. It was Ezra Pound, saying the things he had been saying for thirty years. There was nothing novel about them. Mr. Pound, who had been one of the earliest and one of the most energetic workers in the movement I have been discussing, had himself originated some of these notions, perhaps, but the bulk of them he merely took over whole from what a generation of our literature was saying. I did not need to listen to Ezra Pound for this description of America — I could pick up books in my own library at random and find it nearly anywhere. The base culture, the inferior people, the decadent civilization, the blindness and depravity and disgusting stench of an evil nation, everything that Mr. Pound was saying about us by short wave was at hand in the works of the superior class. The United States government has now formally indicted Mr. Pound for treason. But does not his treason consist of his having had more guts than a good many of his fellow literary men? A number of writers who are on record as believing the same things when the fad was at its height are now on record as rejoicing that he has been pronounced a traitor. Some of the most enthusiastic propagandists of the current literary patriotism, yes and some writers who have somewhat more official positions, heartily believed the same things as Mr. Pound before the going got tough. But they didn't mean what they said? Then Mr. MacLeish is right and they were irresponsible. But they were deceived and have now found the light? That seems a little fragile for seers and prophets, it seems to impair the leadership of letters. But everyone has a right to be wrong? Surely, but it seems to me that Mr. Pound, who kept the courage of his convictions, has a little more dignity even under attainder.

Let us, however, turn from what I have called the official literature of the 1920's — the body of writing which was accepted by most writers as composing the movement, and which was conscious of itself as representing the age. Nothing about the period is more remarkable than the fact that second-rate writers were commonly less susceptible to the literary fallacy than their betters. But I propose to speak of certain first-rate writers who stood outside the movement.

To name only a few, when one comes to Carl Sandburg, E. A. Robinson, Willa Cather, Stephen Vincent Benét, and Robert Frost one enters a world quite different from that of the poets and novelists I have discussed and the critics who made out work-sheets for them. It is certainly not a world sugary or aseptic, washed clean of evil, or emptied of hate, injustice, cruelty, suffering, failure, or decay. No one in the generation has written with fiercer anger of the exploitation of men than Mr. Sandburg. No one in the generation has more witheringly rebuked the ebbing from our consciousness of certain ele-

ments of greatness in our tradition than Miss Cather or
Mr. Benét. In Mr. Frost's poetry there is a resentment of
indignities inflicted on men so fierce that compared to it
Mr. Lewis's protest seems no more than a rowdy bellow
and Mr. Hemingway's a rather craven sob. The difference is not that these writers fail in any way to be aware
of evil or that any of them fail to understand the indecencies of life. It is only a difference of opinion — a difference of opinion about the dignity of man. That is all
but it is a final difference, one that can never be resolved.

The poetry of Robert Frost affirms what the orthodox
literature of the 1920's denies: that human experience
has dignity. Human feeling has finality. Grief may be
hopeless and rebellion may be futile but they are real
and so they are tragic. Tragedy may be immitigable but
it *is* tragedy. The integrity of experience is common to
us all and is sacred in us all. Life *has* sanctity; whether
fulfilled or unfulfilled, it *is* worthy, it *can* be trusted, it
has a dignity that cannot be corrupted. The experience
of men has a fundamental worth which neither other
men, nor God, nor a hostile fate can destroy. Hold the
poems to any light, look at any edge or angle of them,
and they always come to the same focus. A worthless
hired man comes back to an adopted home to die with
people who know his worthlessness. A woman once mad
washes her dishes beside Lake Willoughby in the knowledge of what made her mad and the knowledge that she
will be mad again. A lover of forest orchids whom the
acquisitive society has crippled signs a legal release,

knowing exactly what it was that cut off his feet. In them all is an infrangible dignity. On that infrangible dignity of man Frost's poetry stands foursquare and in Frost's poetry American literature of our time makes its basic affirmation. Man is the measure of things. Man's experience is the measure of reality. Man's spirit is the measure of fate.

The literature we have glanced at lacks this basic acknowledgment of the dignity of man. That is why it is a trivial literature — why the Waste Land of Mr. Eliot and the Solutrean swamp of Mr. Hemingway are less than tragedy, smaller than tragedy. Bulls and male sharks may die in agony, and perhaps there is beauty in the moment of total aggressive force going down before superior force, but though the pain they suffer may shock our nerves we cannot possibly feel their death as tragic. The diminished marionettes of Mr. Dos Passos do not move us to either pain or protest. Conceived as aggregations of reflexes, they lack the humanity which alone gives significance to suffering or cruelty. The frustration of an animal cannot be tragic. The accusation that any man is base or has done evil means nothing at all, unless baseness and evil are defections from the spirit of man. Injustice is an empty word unless man is the measure of justice. There can be no sin unless sin robs man of a state of grace.

That is why so many literary attitudes of our time led eventually to cynicism, heartbreak, or neurotic collapse. Out of them has come much penitence and much of that penitence is merely absurd. It was always possible to inquire "What art?" when someone told us long ago that a spirit bruised by the mediocrity of the life round it intended to seek healing in dedication to beauty. The same question disposes of several dozen literary confessions which have told us that the penitents found no life whatever in beauty, that the palace of art proved to be a house of the dead. Again, those who fled the culture of America, which stifled thought and forbade art and made war on freedom, were presently back from various European Utopias strangely shocked because something Utopian, something which clearly could not be charged against America, had interfered with thought and art and freedom. Another group were betrayed into a more painful bewilderment. They undertook to identify themselves with the workers of the world, only to perish of a dilemma. The blue jeans of the Noble Worker were ceremonial vestments by definition and yet, by earlier definition, the bodies they covered had been denied immortal souls. Three quarters of a literary movement died of internal friction.

Such fragile attitudes are unimportant. They merely move one to inquire whether the lack of intelligence observed was in the culture complained of or in the writers complaining. What counted was not the fragility of small attitudes but the falsity of the fundamental literary attitude. As the catastrophe of our time moved on to its last act, it became clear that literary thinking had got caught in a steel trap of its own making. Literature now found itself summoning men to die for institutions, traditions, possibilities, and hopes which it had lately described as either nonexistent or contemptible. And the men whom it summoned to die for them were the inferior creatures who had lately been incapable even of perceiving, still more of understanding, the values which could make them consent to die.

For it is clear to you that I have been talking about something which need not necessarily be phrased in literary jargon. I have been talking about democracy, I have been talking, in fact, about a very specific form of democracy which first became a faith, first established the tenets and developed the energy of a faith, and first brought that faith to the problems of men living together in society, here in America. It is true that not many writers of the 1920's formally or even consciously opposed democracy. It is proper to remember that a few did. There were some who formally analyzed democracy as a mob of inferior men, dominated by mob lusts and mob panics and conditioned by the swinishness of the average man. Such writers opposed democracy, and so did a number of the period's least stable minds, prettily coquetting with notions of American monarchy and various other lightly literary lunacies, though of course the stampede of literary men to formidable absolutisms, whether communist or fascist, was a phenomenon of the next decade. However, the sum was small and the effect unnoticeable even in the coterie press.

Apart from these, it is just to say that the writers of

the period avowed an honest respect for the word "democracy." A word is only a word, however. American democracy is not a word but American men and women, the beliefs they hold about themselves and one another, institutions they maintain to safeguard their beliefs and to fulfill their hopes, and the goals, ideals, constraints, and prohibitions they share and mutually acknowledge. It was precisely these people and these ideas, feelings, institutions, traditions, and culture which the literature of the period rejected. For these people and their culture the orthodox writers of the period had, as their books prove, an antipathy ranging from mere disillusionment or mere distaste, through hatred, to contempt. No wonder, then, that when judgment day came so incomparably otherwise than Mr. Eliot had predicted, the ideas of many literary men became schizophrenic. Ordinary man must now save the democratic way of life. But one earlier premise held that that way of life was not worth saving. And another earlier premise held that those who must save it could not save it. Either premise seemed to make it impossible to take a stand.

But this merely repeats what I have just said in other words. The Christian view of life holds that men are entitled to primary respect because they are all the children of God — "inasmuch as ye have done it unto one of the least of these my brethren ye have done it unto me." The view of life, Christian or non-Christian, which in all ages is called humanistic holds that man is entitled to primary respect because only in man's consciousness

can the universe be grappled with. And the democratic
view of life holds quite simply that the dignity of man
is unalienable.

But respect for this unalienable dignity is precisely
what had been drained from the literature of the 1920's.
Mr. MacLeish's indictment of modern American literature which I began by quoting says that writers failed
to safeguard our democracy between the two great wars.
There can be no appeal from that judgment. But they
failed to safeguard it because they failed in primary respect for democratic man and primary understanding
of his experience.

I have remarked that for several years now literature
has been confessing its errors. The confession of such
an error as this is a confession of betrayal. It amounts to
a confession that what truly was bankrupt was not
American civilization but the literary way of thinking
about it. That way of thinking, it is now quite clear —
it is temporarily clear even to writers — was not competent to bring in trustworthy findings. It was not an adequate, an accurate, or a dependable instrument. It would
not give results that could be used. The principal effort
of literature has, by its own confession, failed. It has
failed because of the insufficiency of its means. It has
failed because a people, a culture, and a civilization cannot be held to literary values.

V

The Artificers

WE HAVE EXAMINED a complex phenomenon which I have called the literary fallacy. We have most often examined it in the attempt of writers to evalue American life as a whole. We have found the common denominator of a good many discordant minds in the fact that they work from a body of general ideas which are organized in systems. These thinkers are, I believe, the only ones who have made the whole range of American life their province. Certainly they are the only ones who have tried to pass absolute judgments on it. Most of them begin with the study of literature; most of them employ literary data exclusively. Practically all of them who extend their inquiry beyond literary data extend it by means of primarily literary ideas.

All of them, however, have to use such words as "culture" and "civilization." I have pointed out that some of them mean by culture simply the writing of books and associated activities. Some who have meant more than that have left their conceptions of culture unstated and we have had to infer what they were. Now "culture" is a word which other kinds of thinkers must also use. An anthropologist, for instance, may speak of "a culture" but he tends to avoid absolutes, he does not make final value-judgments. Furthermore, his "culture" includes many interests and pursuits which are excluded from the meaning of the word as systematic literary thinking has usually employed it.

We have reached a point where it is desirable to glance at certain activities which have been excluded from the literary conception of culture. There are a very great many of them but I have time to discuss only two. These two are not explicitly included in the criticism I have dealt with here; I have faithfully searched it for any implicit inclusion but have not found it. They are not cultural activities according to the literary systems which have undertaken to appraise American life.

A certain captain of artillery lost his right arm at the battle of Shiloh. His name was John Wesley Powell. In civil life he had been a schoolmaster and an amateur naturalist. He fought through the rest of the war and at its end was mustered out with the rank of major; throughout his life his associates referred to him as "the Major." He was soon attracted to a new kind of career which the end of the war had made possible. Up to that time the vast national domain lying west of the Missouri River had been explored only haphazardly. No systematic study of it had been begun or even conceived. Private enterprises such as fur companies, mining companies, and railroad companies had surveyed parts of it. The engineer and topographical corps of the army had surveyed other parts and made limited studies; the best of these had been made in the prewar surveys for the Pacific railroad. Such work was valuable but exceedingly little of it had had any social purpose and the entire sum of it was small. The national domain had not been studied as a whole, it had not been mapped, its natural resources had not been appraised. Except in the most trivial superficialities, no effort had been made to understand its possibilities for American society or to work out the conditions which it would impose on its future inhabitants. The national government turned to this immense work as soon as the Civil War ended. Still administering some of the surveys through the War Department but employing such other agencies as the Department of the Interior and the Smithsonian Institution, it set out to bring the national domain under control of full and exact knowledge. This was an inspiring undertaking and it fired the imagination of Major Powell. He joined the undertaking and spent the rest of his life working as a part of it.

Powell was the most notable of a number of notable men who devoted themselves to this study. He headed what was called the Geographical and Geological Survey of the Rocky Mountain Region. Ferdinand Vandiveer Hayden was at the head of the Geological Survey of the Territories. There were two other surveys and at the head of the one called the Geological Exploration of the Fortieth Parallel was Clarence King. Systematic criticism knows that King wrote excellent prose, had a scandal in his private life, and (when this mood is on the critic) may be considered one more artist crushed by our acquisitive society because he suffered a nervous breakdown and sometimes worked for mining corporations. But in the entire literary examination of American culture there is, so far, not a single effort to so much as state the importance of King's work in that culture. Nor have I found in it any mention of Powell, Hayden, or such associates of theirs as G. K. Gilbert, A. H. Thompson, and Clarence Dutton. The work these men did and the institutions they founded, which have been serving our civilization for seventy years, must be either unknown to the appraisers of that civilization or considered culturally unimportant.

John Wesley Powell was a heroic figure. His personal courage was great. He led the first expedition that navigated the Green and Colorado Rivers; the story of his two trips down those canyons is a chapter in our book of stirring deeds. The stump of his amputated arm caused him periodic suffering all through his life, but the one-armed man climbed the cliffs and peaks of the region he made his own and no sentence he ever wrote suggests that the cripple felt himself under any handicap. In a period when the Americans were exhibiting a talent for organization amounting to a national genius, his skill as an organizer was outstanding. His was the conception and his the energy that unified the study of the national domain, bringing the four separate surveys together and founding the permanent Geological Survey. Clarence King, its first director, served for a year; Powell succeeded him and held the directorship for fourteen years. The Geological Survey had in due course to study the Indians. Powell took a young science which had been exclusively a private pursuit of individual scholars, organized and systematized it, dedicated a new department of the national government to it, founded journals and other means of publication, and in short organized an entire field. He was one of the first great anthropologists and his vision and energy created the Bureau of American Ethnology, which he directed for more than twenty years. Again, since his lifework was devoted to the arid regions of the national domain, he had to deal with the problems of their use. Among those problems the foremost one was the cultivation of arid lands. It was Powell who conceived that society itself must be responsible for the preservation and development of their wealth, and for this conception he fought heroically throughout his life. When someone gets round to writing his biography this part of it will tell a story of hard struggle against the forces of private exploitation, confused state and national interests, scandal, libel, and the ruthless drive of industry and finance of the time — a struggle in which he was partly defeated and partly triumphant. What came out of it was in many respects different from what he fought for, and yet he is the true begetter of the Reclamation Service.

Powell was influential in the founding or the development of the Forest Service, the National Park Service,
and several learned societies, and his work led directly
to such other institutions as the Bureau of Mines. But
let us consider the three I have named, the Geological
Survey, the Bureau of Ethnology, and the Reclamation
Service. The first two became national in scope but, with
the third, they were founded in relation to the unoc-
cupied national domain. It was an area of incalculable
wealth and it now supports a population of many millions. When the American people reached it in their
westward passage, they encountered conditions of geography and climate which set new terms for the processes
of life. The methods which had served for the occupation of the continent up to then could not meet the new
conditions. American culture had to develop new ways
of dealing with its environment, conforming to it, and
existing in it. As Powell wrote: —

> The physical conditions which exist in that land,
> and which inexorably control the operations of men,
> are such that the industries of the West are neces-
> sarily unlike those of the East, and their institutions
> must be adapted to their industrial wants. It is thus
> that a new phase of Aryan civilization is being de-
> veloped in the western half of America.

A new phase of civilization, with indigenous institutions, has now been developing in the West for seventy
years. It has had to modify many fundamental concep-

tions which the Americans who went West took with them. Even law, which is the expression of institutional habits, has changed — slowly, with a conservatism that has frequently had large parts of a population actually living outside the law, but basically. Land is not held in the West in the same terms that control its ownership elsewhere. The law of water right is altogether different. Co-operative social institutions of kinds new to American culture have developed there. Some portions of the area had to be withdrawn from any exploitation, private or state, for the sake of the future of the nation as a whole. Other areas and other kinds of wealth had to be withdrawn from private ownership and state control, to be administered by the federal government which alone could equitably develop them. Others had to be made a charge of the national government because only the nation could finance their development. Many ways of thinking about ownership, development, and administration had to be changed fundamentally before the modern West could exist.

But there are matters even more basic than these: methods of determining the fitness of various kinds of land for various uses, kinds of wealth, kinds of crops, fit species of plants, fit species of animals, methods of farming and ranching, proportionate relationships of crops, technologies of farming, kinds and proportions of industries, technologies of industry, institutions of social control, kinds of schools, kinds of taxation, technologies of communication, adjustments of classes and individuals, adjustments of interests, adjustments of common rights and individual rights — an almost infinite number of new adaptations necessitated by the new conditions of life. The culture of millions of Americans has developed through these adaptations.

There is not one of them which the three institutions Powell founded or, with his associates, begot — there is not one of them which the three institutions have not affected. They have had a fundamental place in the development of the West and in the lives of everyone who lives there now or has lived there in seventy years. They are fundamental in the fact that millions of people can live in the West at all, and the life of everyone who lives there is in part shaped by them every day. One thinks of the Geological Survey. It explored the national domain, mapped it, developed exact knowledge of its climate and rainfall and all other basic conditions, surveyed its resources in timber and minerals and oil, in agricultural and grazing wealth. It derived exact knowledge on the basis of which private enterprise could act, the federal government could preserve, develop, and increase our national resources, Congress and state legislatures could base regulations of control, and at any moment the present of American life could act on behalf of the future. All this in immediate, practical application to the conditions of life in the West. But also its surveys and discoveries, its maps and records, its papers and monographs and reports, have steadily enriched the common culture of mankind. If the Geological Survey has been of incalculable practical importance to the United States, it has also been, ever since its foundation, one of the vital sources of human knowledge.

One thinks of the Bureau of Ethnology. When it was founded anthropology was an eclectic study, a pursuit of amateurs. From its foundation the Bureau has played a leading part in the development of the science of anthropology, one of the fruitful sciences of the modern world. It too has been a generative influence in the common culture of mankind.

One thinks of the Reclamation Service — how additional millions may live in Los Angeles, how crops may grow in the Imperial Valley and innumerable other places where once crops could not grow, how magnesium may be made in the Nevada desert, how millions of horsepower may be generated at Grand Coulee, how alfalfa or fruit trees now make alive the once dead land of the alkali desert, how the immemorial effort of men to master their environment has succeeded in hundreds of thousands of square miles because the Reclamation Service found the knowledge and put it to work. What is culture? What is civilization?

Surely the hundreds of men who have spent their lives in these three agencies increasing knowledge, putting knowledge to work, and enhancing the life not only of the United States but of all nations — surely here for seventy years, and ignored by literary folk for seventy years, has been a living culture, *sub specie aeternitatis*, of which the nation that it expressed must be proud.

So one comes back to Powell, whose genius, vision, energy, and courage created these three agencies. His shadow is long. In his own right he was a distinguished geologist and anthropologist. He gave both sciences not only great problems to solve, which is one measure of greatness in any science, but also fundamental ideas, some of them revolutionary, which are working for both sciences still. It would be pleasant to say more about such things but I prefer to end with another aspect of his genius, the literary aspect. For this man wrote many scientific and philosophical papers and he wrote books, one of which we must glance at, his *Report on the Lands of the Arid Region of the United States*. Mr. Brooks has not heard about it, nor Mr. Mumford, Mr. Stearns, Mr. Lewisohn, Mr. Frank, Mr. Parrington, or Mr. Hicks, nor even Mr. Edmund Wilson or Mr. Kazin. It does not lie within the awareness of Mr. Lewis's University or Winnemac and it would go unnoticed in the dawn-man jungle where Mr. Hemingway's anthropoids bellow and whimper. In a word, it is not literature.

It is only a book about a land and a people by one of the men whom Dante and Virgil found in an eternity of their own kind, the masters of those who know. It is basic, it is original, it is unique, and it is, in the strictest sense of a badly misused word, revolutionary. It deals with the arid West, four tenths of the United States. Of this vast area Powell was truly a discoverer, in that the knowledge which he acquired in years of preparation for this book was the first accurate knowledge of it. He was an innovator, a pioneer, a prime mover, bringing precise instruments of knowledge for the first time to a great subject, and endeavoring to make those instruments serve society. He was the first and he put his knowledge into a book that is fundamental for society — fundamental and permanent. The book discovers, determines, and states the conditions which must govern life and institutions as the American people shall occupy their national domain. Stated in it are the revolutionary changes which law, ownership, administration, commerce, industry, farming, and ranching must undergo in adaptation to the conditions of life. The bases of administration, control, co-operation, prohibition, and sanction on which the institutions must eventually be grounded are also stated — and many of the failures that have occurred on the way to realizing them are forecast. You can find there many predictions since verified — the war of private interests, the jealousies of the states, the coming of the Dust Bowl. You can find completely stated at the very beginning of the era the program of administration which has been worked out experimentally and laboriously, after vast waste, with great suffering and injustice, through seventy years — which even now has not yet achieved all that Powell foresaw as necessary in 1878.

In short here is a vision of society. It is not a vision composed out of abstract logic and beautiful thought. It is one which exists in and as knowledge, rigorously determined, rigorously applied. It is true as science is true, for sixty-five years of human life have verified it. It is true as great imagination is true, for, not content with the inert phenomena of science, it works habitually with human consciousness, human energies, and their living interaction with nature. It has shaped institutions and the lives of millions of people. It is generative, it has brought forth fruit, it has proved creative. It is permanent in American life, a monument of human greatness.

The dedicated literary intelligence of our time ventured to pass judgment on American life without taking into account such men as Powell and such institutions as the Geological Survey. The literary intelligence did not know that such men and such institutions existed. Its judgments were ignorant. They were also arrogantly naïve, dilettante, arty, and a little epicene. Who licensed literary men to be ignorant of the things they presumed to judge?

These men and their work belonged originally to a period which systematic thinking has fitted into another cliché, the Gilded Age. You will remember that the Literary Credo sees American life of that period as a swinish snouting at the trough; the sensitive awareness of writers finds nothing there which writers can, in the words of one of the most celebrated, regard without a shudder. So let us turn to the decade we have been concerned with, the Age of Harding and Coolidge. In the Literary Credo it is tawdry, venal, and corrupt, its culture barren, its life contemptible. It is the era of Gopher Prairie, the typist home at teatime and the small house agent's clerk, Mr. Mencken's booboisie, Mr. Heming-way's *castrati*, Mr. Jeffers's less kindly wolves — the age which Mr. Geismar sums up in a pretty psalm made up of pretty clichés trustfully borrowed from the manufacturers of clichés. Conceivably something of that age also may have been outside the literary awareness.

For a college audience it would be appropriate to mention the labors of many thousands of unremarkable men and women who during the 1920's remade the educational systems of the United States, from the kindergartens to the graduate schools, immensely improving the education open to you beyond what was provided for my generation. This work was, I believe, cultural but you will find it ignored by the literary view or mentioned only with derision. Or it is tempting to tolerate the profit motive and suggest that business, the blackest villain of the Twenties, may have been cultural. We have lately realized that to organize the flow of vegetables so that such a city as New York may count on eating, or to organize the flow of fuel oil so that such a city as Boston may keep warm, requires a high degree of civilization. Some of the technologists and industrial scientists whom you will not find mentioned in systematic criticism, and some of the manufacturers of gadgets whom you will find mentioned, were also, it may be, enlarging the cultural heritage.

Or I might mention a field of activity closer to my own interests, the state historical societies. Many of them, of course, have been active agents in our culture for several generations, but it is fair to say that for many of them the Twenties marked the first intelligent and sustained effort to bring the study of local history above the level of piety. Before 1920 the historical society of my native state, for instance, hardly engaged in anything more useful than ancestor worship, but since then it has conducted a mature study of the state's past. Professor R. C. Buley of this University has lately noted a similar development in the Indiana Historical Society, under his old teacher Dr. Esarey, and I have personal reasons for mentioning the Illinois State Historical Society and, collaterally, *The Centennial History of Illinois*. It is not the state historical societies only but many other organizations which during the Twenties worked honorably in the American past, studying our history and folklore, building up a great treasury of material. There is something immensely comic in remembering that this work, done by quite ordinary people all over the country, was really the search for a "usable past" which systematic criticism supposed it was making — but which it made by sitting quietly on its hams and thinking hard. The dedicated intelligence was reporting that we had no past, but thousands of men and women were tranquilly finding out what it was. They were building up the cultural heritage.

A good many kinds of people who were denied literary approval during the Twenties would serve my demurrer, in fact, but I choose to look at a single small part of Dr. Martin Arrowsmith's profession.

Unassisted by the respect of systematic critics, laboratory and clinical medicine and the related sciences — surgery, public health, epidemiology, bacteriology, and the like — made more progress during the 1920's than in any quarter century, yes, any century, before. In 1930 medicine was a new world, changed fundamentally from what it had been in 1920, remade by the work of thousands of men and women, and some of mankind's oldest fears had been ended forever, and there was a promise of future achievements even more dazzling. Such progress, I think, is not unrelated to the human spirit. It is entitled to respect as culture. I select a single development. I select this particular one because, on the one hand, no foundation subsidized the researches and, on the other, no single lightning-flash like the discovery of insulin or of the cure for pernicious anemia expedited them. The development occurred inside the republic of medicine — where genius is much less common than in literature — and it came from the ordinary labor of medical men working at their jobs.

So long as there have been men on earth, and since long before they learned the use of fire, men have been dying of burns. So long as there have been physicians, the treatment of burns has been a routine problem of every practitioner. Suffering from burns is one of the most common and most painful of human ills, and death from burns is one of the most terrible. Deaths from burns are so numerous that they have long been accepted as one of the permanent hazards of everyday life, just as we have accepted the mortality of traffic accidents. From eight to ten thousand people die of burns in the United States every year. In an average year perhaps a thousand die of infantile paralysis, which, compared with burns, is not a killer since only about five per cent of those affected by it die and only about ten per cent are crippled. In 1940 more people were killed by burns in the United States than by bombing in England.

In 1920 medical science had been dealing with burns for about twenty-five hundred years. In all that time it had had to confine its efforts to easing the pain of burns. In folk medicine, in magical and empirical medicine, there is likely to be a grain of hard truth in practices which are crusted over with ignorance or superstition. One physician, you will remember, analyzed an old wife's brew which was reputed to cure heart disease, and from its fifty-seven varieties of yarbs isolated digitalis. Similarly, as far back as the sixth century before Christ, Chinese physicians were, as one of many ways of treating burns, applying poultices of tea leaves. They were really using tannic acid, though their hypotheses were ridiculous — as all medical explanations of burns continued to be down almost to 1900 — and tannic acid is still widely used, though perhaps not always wisely used, in the treatment of burns.

The point is that, whether folklore, magic, superstition, science, or the empirical procedure of your family doctor, all that medicine could do was to treat the pain of a burn. Through twenty-five hundred years of treating burns, no one knew what a person whom a burn killed had died of. Medicine knew only that a patient of whose body surface more than a third was burned would surely die. Primitive man in his caves had known as much. Hippocrates, Galen, and the Arab physicians had known it. The nineteenth century had developed its majestic discoveries in physiology and bacteriology but the basic knowledge of burns remained what it had been in Galen's time, and a physician of 1900 hurrying to the bedside of a person who had suffered a large burn knew that his patient must die. The medical literature which that physician might consult was still, in the light of what we now know about burns, quite as irrelevant, quite as helplessly lost in folklore and guess, as anything in the preceding centuries.

Historians sometimes speak of a law of multiple invention, by which they mean that the general cultural climate reaches a stage where a number of men will go looking for the answer to the same question, and when the instruments of knowledge have developed to a point where they can find it, perhaps simultaneously and with no knowledge of one another's search. Toward 1900 something like this began to happen in the study of burns. Physicians began to be dissatisfied with the accepted hypotheses and with the general state of knowledge. Just what killed the patient who died of a burn? Could not the patient with a major burn be saved? Their researches were unorganized but at last they began to develop theories about burns. One theory held that the skin was a vital organ and that when too much of it had been destroyed, the patient must die. Another held that the action of heat formed specific poisons, such as ptomaines for instance, in the skin and that these were absorbed and killed the patient. Another held that the patient died of concentration of the blood, the plasma having shifted from the bloodstream to the area of the burn. And so on. A variety of theories developed but through the first twenty-odd years of this century medicine did not devise techniques of research which could reject the false or sift out from it what might be elements of the truth.

Then in the 1920's the fundamental problems of burns were solved. When the decade began, hospitals were still losing upwards of thirty per cent of all burn cases brought to them, which meant that all patients with major burns were dying. It was still the hard empirical belief of medicine that burns of one-third the body surface or more were fatal. By 1930 that belief and expectation had been completely overturned. I cannot outline the many researches which led to that result but will mention three decisive steps.

In 1925 Dr. E. C. Davidson of Detroit published his findings about the tannic-acid treatment of burns which he had developed. This treatment has since been in great part superseded but it was a remarkable advance, and the important thing is that, in developing it, Dr. Davidson had taken the fundamental step of organizing a *team* for the treatment of burns. When a burned patient was brought to his hospital — it was the Henry Ford Hospital — he was taken in charge by a team who worked, step by step, as carefully and systematically as a surgical team working on a brain tumor. For the first time treatment was methodized, systematized, and conducted with scientific procedure. There was a drop in the mortality of burns and many badly burned patients recovered. Furthermore, the horrible and horrifying suffering of the burned patient was ended. He spent his days and nights comfortably, not in the screaming agony to which physicians had been hardened for twenty-five hundred years.

In 1926 and 1927 came the findings of Dr. F. P. Underhill of New Haven. Essentially his work consisted of shock therapy. There had always been a heavy mortality during the first three days after the burn. These patients had been dying of shock, precisely the same shock that any other kind of injury produces. Medicine had assumed that there was some intrinsic, specific kind of shock peculiar to burns and had variously explained it — as, for instance, that it was caused by the absorption of a poison. Dr. Underhill's researches demonstrated its true nature. He treated it by replacement therapy, injecting fluids intravenously to replace the plasma that had been drawn from the body to the burn. This treatment greatly reduced the mortality of the first three days. Medicine now understood that the early deaths were due to shock and so could prevent them.

But what about the patients who died after the phase

of shock had ended? Underhill's work had proved that they did not die of something absorbed by the body from the burn, that in fact the absorption was in the other direction. It became clear to Dr. Robert H. Aldrich of the Johns Hopkins that one fundamental study had never been made. For twenty-five hundred years burns had been producing pus but no one had ever analyzed the pus. Dr. Aldrich began making cultures at four-hour intervals and found that all burns showed the same phenomena. For the first forty hours the pus contained a mixture of all kinds of bacteria. Then the streptococcus began to outgrow all the other organisms, killing them and replacing them. At the end of seventy-two hours the burn was bathed in a pus of virulent streptococcus, the same organism that produces the "strep" throat, pneumonia, peritonitis, and so on. Dr. Aldrich's findings were confirmed by work done at the Royal Infirmary of Glasgow. So a wholly new theory was formulated: that the burned patient who had survived the shock died of infection.

On the basis of this theory, Dr. Aldrich evolved a new treatment. He sterilized the burned surface, using a well-known antiseptic, an aniline dye called gentian violet, which is nontoxic to humans but kills the streptococcus. It converts the upper layer of the burn to a parchment-like substance, which stops pain entirely and acts as a scaffolding for new skin to grow on. In the first year during which the gentian violet treatment was used at Johns Hopkins, the mortality of burns dropped from forty-two per cent to twelve per cent. In the second year it dropped to five per cent.

Since 1930 much more work has been done, notably the experiments with the sulfa drugs. The war has greatly stimulated research because so many combatants are suffering major burns. At this moment many researches are under way, particularly in the physiology of burns. Future study will probably deal with ways of more completely sterilizing the burned surface and with refining the techniques of plastic surgery in order to prevent deformities and scars. Since medicine does not now anticipate that it will ever be possible to graft the skin of one person on another person, it seems likely that the totally burned patient, the person whose entire skin area has been destroyed, can never be saved. It seems likely also that the present mortality rate, which is the one achieved during the 1920's, will not be materially lowered.

But because of the work done during the 1920's the problem is solved. Medicine is no longer afraid of burns. In 1920 thirty per cent of all burned patients brought to hospitals died, all large burns were fatal, and there was no hope of saving any patient if he had a burn involving one third of the body surface or more. Today no more than five per cent of burns are fatal. The large burn has lost its terror. Many men and women who had burns of two thirds of the skin area, and who in 1920 would infallibly have died, are completely cured, restored to health and effectiveness, doing their jobs and living satisfying lives.

That is: in ten years medicine found ways of coming to grips with a problem which it had previously been unable to solve. In ten years the problem yielded to research and the mystery was dispelled. Fundamental ignorance was transformed to fundamental knowledge. Medicine learned what a burn does to the tissues and mechanism of the body and therefore how it may be treated. One more gap in medical knowledge, one of the oldest and most obdurate gaps, was closed.

These events took place in the society of medical men. That society is part of the larger society, and those events were a function of the general culture. In the ten-year research I have briefly described there were, of course, many false leads, mistaken investigations, fallacious hypotheses, wasted experiments, blind alleys, misinterpreted results, and wholly erroneous ideas. Certainly there were also rivalries. It may be that there were charlatanism, publicity, and controversy which resembled literary charlatanism, publicity, and controversy in failing to confer dignity on the participants. Nevertheless the researches led to usable results which increased knowledge. The events took place in a free society, not formally organized but close-knit and co-operative. Whatever the rivalries of theory or research, the methods, ideas, and results of every investigator were open to all. A researcher in San Francisco had at his disposal the work being done at Portland, San Antonio, Chicago, Philadelphia, and every other place where doctors were studying burns. The progress of a research in Baltimore could be used in a research in St. Louis which may have been intended to disprove its findings. There was an interchange of work and ideas toward a social end.

Moreover, though our San Francisco researcher may have been working on only a minute part of the problem of burns, or perhaps on something that was only incidental to the problem, he had at his disposal not only the work of all others who were working on burns but much else as well. He could call on the hospitals, the medical societies, the great foundations supported by corrupt billionaires, the Public Health Service, other departments of state and national governments, and those monsters of greed which made Professor Gottlieb's life a long frustration, the manufacturers of drugs and medicines. With the most diverse motives, some of them doubtless unlovely, all such agencies were at his service, usable in the solution of his problem. This was not a directed co-operation for the increase of knowledge but certainly it was an effective one. Finally, a researcher in San Francisco walked in step with the development of all medicine and the related sciences. Year by year he could bring to bear on the physiology or the bacteriology or the therapy of burns the results of thousands of researches in other fields. As a worker in medicine he was a citizen of medical society and, as such, he was a citizen of the republic of learning.

The story of burns is one small part of the story of medicine in the 1920's. Looking back over the annals of American medicine in that decade, one feels that it opened a finer era in human life. Mysteries that had balked medicine throughout history were solved. The area of human knowledge and therefore of human control was greatly expanded. Some kinds of suffering and some kinds of death were mastered. Afflictions of entire populations were reduced. The hope of ordinary people everywhere to live more comfortably, with less pain, with better functioning, was increased. Whether in the control of infection, the control of epidemics, the deficiency diseases, nutrition, surgery, anesthesia, childbirth, endocrinology, psychiatry — wherever you approach medicine you see that you have entered a new era of human knowledge. The general cultural heritage has been so enriched that mankind is able to deal with some of its eternal problems more effectively than, up to then, anyone had dared to think possible.

To work toward the conquest of pain, toward the reduction of fear and crippling and unnecessary death, toward the enhancement of human functioning, toward the expansion of knowledge — I suppose that to work toward such ends is not ignoble. Medical men have never widely considered themselves a superior class, and certainly no one who knows them well has ever so considered them. Original sin has not been washed from them. The profession as a whole, its members, its general ideas, its specific ideas, can be arranged in the bell-shaped curve that describes the rest of us. Look at any given medical scientist of the period, or at any given moment of the science, and there is a fair chance that you will see nothing in particular to rejoice about. But look at the ten years of medicine, the 1920's in America, and you are looking at one of history's heroic ages.

This conquest of ignorance was forced to proceed without the attention of the literary folk who for the common good undertook to determine the worth of American civilization. I have remarked that you cannot find John Wesley Powell in the critical systems. Likewise it is not important to the systems that medicine was constructing a new world. Systematic criticism assigned no value to such kinds of creation. If it had undertaken to pass judgment anyone could have worked out its answer in advance, just as its answer would have been worked out in advance. During the 1920's it would have said that medical research was not a truly cultural activity, since it did not deal with letters or leadership or beauty or the imagination — just as during the 1930's it would have said that medicine was a particularly reactionary phase of capitalistic decay. At neither time would it have been troubled by the fact that pernicious anemia could now be cured or that knowledge had been increased.

The medical sciences are a single item. One thinks of other sciences which, during the 1920's, show much the same picture — the laboratories of universities, foundations, and large industries in which thousands of not very remarkable men were laboriously tending the frontiers of knowledge, adding to the reservoir of power by which the generations increase our control of nature, remaking what is known and thought. One thinks of the "pure" sciences and of the technologies. One thinks of such humble agencies as the Bureau of Public Roads. I could take particular pleasure in describing still another kind of effort and, as I referred to the Geological Survey during the Gilded Age, should like to outline what the Department of Agriculture did during the 1920's for the enhancement of American life.

Such energies as these exist as parts of a culture. The parts are mutually interdependent, they exist because of one another, they work in relation to one another, and certainly the vigor of the parts depends on and attests the health of the whole. If pernicious anemia is cured, if the aberrations of light are determined, if pellagra is all but stamped out, if the spectra of stars are analyzed, if a larger percentage of men and women go to college, if the enjoyment of music ceases to be a caste privilege, all such things occur in relation to the culture of a people. When you look at such parts of a people's culture you do not see the mediocre mob working enviously to base ends that systematic criticism described. Neither, in a later idiom, do you see a sick society dying convulsively — or how was the society able to resist the catastrophes of the 1930's and on what do we depend to take it through the universal war of the 1940's?

By what warrant did literary men presume to report such judgments when, in Mr. Wilson's observation, they attacked the life of their time more unanimously than any other writers in any period of history? By what sanction is the writer of a book on America's coming-of-age, or a book on character and opinion in the United States, or a book on the promise of American life, or a book on the golden day — by what sanction is an embroiderer of literary idea permitted to judge a nation's intelligence working with the conditions of its life, before he has consulted the evidence? By what authority are writers whose vocation apparently requires them to be ignorant of culture permitted to be critics of culture?

We have thus come back to a familiar fact: the repudiation of American life by American literature during the 1920's signified that writers were isolated or insulated from the common culture. There is something intrinsically absurd in the image of a literary man informing a hundred and twenty million people that their ideals are base, their beliefs unworthy, their ideas vulgar, their institutions corrupt, and, in sum, their civilization too trivial to engage that literary man's respect. That absurdity is arrogant but also it is naïve and most of all it is ignorant. For the repudiation was the end-product of systems of thinking, and the systems arose in an ignorance that extended to practically everything but imaginative literature and critical comment on it. Systematic critics, that is, worked heroically in the books of novelists, poets, and one another and disregarded nearly everything else. No doubt in one light they exhibit an exalted devotion to pure thought, but in another light they exhibit the odd spectacle of the literary intelligence committing suicide.

VI

The Meal in the Firkin

~~~~~~

ARLY in this discussion I quoted a passage from Van Wyck Brooks in which he attacked contemporary literature on the ground that it was out of touch with the primary experiences of life. When that denunciation appeared the coteries counterattacked. Mr. T. S. Eliot, for instance, replied that Mr. Brooks ought to have devoted himself, not to assailing those who had borne the battle with him, but to inquiring why the literature he now attacked was what it was. The proper question, that is to say, is not whether the typist home at teatime and the young man carbuncular truly represent life in the modern world but, rather, how Mr. Eliot, a writer, came to think that they truly represent it. Mr. Eliot's transposition moves inside the literary fallacy.

The title of Oswald Spengler's phantasy of doom was incorrectly rendered in the American translation. Spengler was writing of the downfall of the West, not the decline of the West. It seems likely that the dilemma which produced his phantasy was of the German landowning class, not of the sunset lands as a whole — that when war brought our Western cultures to one kind of test their response overturned his vision. It seems likely also that the majestic processes of erosion with which Spengler dealt cannot be adequately studied in, for instance, *Main Street* or *The Sun Also Rises*. At any rate, I prefer to postpone such a study and, instead, to allude briefly to a few, a very few, of the events that occurred in the United States during a generation or two before the literature we have been dealing with.

Henry Adams hungered and thirsted after unity. When at last he took instruction from Samuel Langley and Willard Gibbs, he found it in the mathematics of physical force. In the outcome, however, the man of pure thought did not understand Gibbs. He failed to understand the prime quality of an equilibrium of forces, which is that the forces composing the equilibrium are mutually dependent. A radical error of the literary thinking we deal with has been the same unawareness of the mutual dependence of phenomena. Adams's thesis proved powerfully attractive to literary minds; it moved by means of symbols and it produced absolutes. And also it had a further seductiveness: Adams believed that a social energy is a physical energy and can be expressed mathematically. He believed that men grow progressively unhappier in accordance with the law of bodies falling without friction through space. I am not aware that any physical scientist has accepted his premises or confirmed his conclusions. By laborious and exquisite calculations his perturbed mind sought the Virgin of Chartres in the displacement of steam by the energy of expanding gases and by the discharge of electric potentials. We are involved with intricate metaphors and we must not for a moment forget that they are metaphors but, granting Adams the privilege of speaking within them, we must concede him a valid observation. He observed that the Civil War accelerated the momentum of events.

One necessary way of looking at the Civil War — it is by no means the most important way but it is necessary — is to observe that a high-energy system triumphed over a low-energy system, thus freeing itself to more efficient functioning. Slave power yielded to machine power. Machine power increased and has gone on increasing. Year by year more horsepower per capita came to exist — to do the work of the United States. To create wealth. To manufacture, improve, diversify, and cheapen goods. To modify old ways of life and to create new ones. Some parts of the United States were almost completely industrialized, some slowly and only a little, but there was no part which the expanding industry did not alter. Innumerable handicrafts disappeared; many old trades were revolutionized, many new ones evolved. Vast shifts in wealth, vast changes in the proportions of wealth, of population, and of social classes were always in process. Constantly, the reservoir of surplus, available power increased. Constantly, new sources and new applications of power were being developed. New kinds of power were being utilized. It is true that electricity and the internal-combustion engine were in conflict with steam, as Adams perceived; but also they were added to steam, increasing the reservoir of available power. The society based on the expanding industry was necessarily fluid, changeable, full of interior movements and conflicts of its own, always adjusting and always changing — changing with an accelerating, sometimes catastrophic speed.

Two things must be said. First, the social equilibrium of the United States was an unstable equilibrium, always in passage from one state to another. The strains put on it were gigantic. Sometimes they seemed certain to capsize the equilibrium but always they were contained. The dissolution never quite occurred. The new state was always established and began to shift toward the next state — and always the reservoir of surplus, available power increased. Second, on the whole, in the average, across the years, and considering all classes, the increase of mechanical power steadily lifted the standard of living. That part of the American promise which offered mankind more abundant food and greater comfort than men had ever had elsewhere was steadily fulfilled.

Observe that, already, we have had to strain at our metaphors. When we speak of steam, or electricity, or expanding gases, we are speaking literally, in terms commensurable with Gibbs, of measurable quantities — that is, of real energies. But when we speak of a social equilibrium we have ceased to speak of real energies; we have begun to speak figuratively. We must now go on to speak of other kinds of influence that were at work on

American life at the same time, and when we call them energies we are speaking even more metaphorically. They are incommensurable with steam.

The farther Middle West and the Far West filled up. Minnesota, Nebraska, western Kansas, western Texas, the Dakotas, Colorado, Oregon, Washington, Utah, Idaho, New Mexico, Arizona, Oklahoma, Wyoming, Montana. The entire agricultural system was fundamentally changed, again with great dislocations of the general equilibrium. Railroads pushed across the new states. New counties, new villages, new towns, new cities developed. Relations of section to section and class to class were in process of continuous change. The good homestead land was used up; homesteaders worked on into marginal lands, into grazing lands, into arid lands. Finally the population of the West reached such a concentration that the technical term "frontier" no longer applied to it. This was a finality. Our oldest tradition, our most powerful social force, had, technically, reached its end.

Besides the Americans who thus put new strains on the equilibrium by moving from old lands to new, hundreds of thousands of immigrants came from Europe to the new states. They were mainly northern European, though a few came from every country. Meanwhile a new immigration was going on, from eastern, central, and southern Europe. Italians, Poles, Czechs, Slavs, a variety of others, were added to the melting pot. These joined the city proletariat or went into the basic industries like steel, wherever located. The racial stock of the United States was changing radically.

Another fundamental shift was the urbanization of the United States. Towns were growing into cities, cities were growing into big cities, big cities were growing into metropolises. The percentage of Americans who lived in cities steadily increased, until in our own time it grew larger than the percentage of those who lived in villages and the country. That fact meant another change of final importance, like the end of the frontier. Every conceivable human adaptation, habit, custom, and way of living was modified by this shift. Suburban areas developed. Whole sections of states and eventually whole states declined in population. Whole aggregations of agriculture, of commerce, of production were depressed. Congeries of mores, values, and beliefs were altered. New forms of distribution and supply were developed. Enormous series of interactions were set in new directions.

To capitalize the new wealth and the new power, to organize an industry that was almost beyond control, a new financial system was developing. Segments of industry warred on one another and began to consolidate as trusts. Trusts warred on one another and began to consolidate as what is called — none too accurately — finance capitalism. Financial and social upheavals attended every stage of the process. In effect, finance took over industry; if it tended to rationalize industry, it meanwhile subjugated agriculture on behalf of industry. High tariffs and open immigration buttressed the consolidation, and forty years of Greenbackery, Grangerism, and Populism attested the turmoil of whole sections. And yet even the financial equilibrium was unstable, always working out new shapes, proportions, and phases. It was composed of various interests, sections, and classes, and these were in tension one with another. New orientations, new struggles, new dislocations were in process.

Meanwhile the South, whose social system had been destroyed by the Civil War, was building a new one, handicapped by the debris of the old system, the overturn of classes, political subjugation, the extinction of wealth. The agonizing process was made no easier by the fact that the experience of defeat was pushing the social myths entirely out of touch with reality. Meanwhile also the social system of the Middle West went on working out its own specific adaptations, adjustments, and orientations. The development of the Middle West as an organized system within the American system is one of the fundamental facts not only of the United States but of the modern world. For fifty years it had been clear that the Mississippi Valley must eventually be the dominant culture of the United States. Following the Civil War, the institutions and economy that must eventually produce that dominance began to reveal their shape.

I describe a nation animated by the gigantic forces of the second half of the nineteenth century, moving at vast speed through rapidly shortening changes of phase. The accelerating physical energies of American industrialism, the enhanced human energies of a free social system, the energies of potential in the national resources, were transforming the nation continuously. While the nineteenth century was running out, they were inexorably advancing it toward world power. As early as 1847, for instance, they had made clear that there would never again be a peacetime famine in the Western world.

Such things enlarged men's consciousness. Space shrank and man had a new freedom — to cross this continent in a week, then in four days, then in ten hours, whereas his father had crossed it in six or seven months. To get a letter from his son in twenty-four hours instead of as many days. To visit with his mother over a week end, a thousand miles away. To pick up a telephone and hear a voice which, a generation earlier, he might not have heard for years. To move about at his need or even his whim. The automobile soon made space merely the arc of time's chord, and presently the airplane came close to obliterating it. The season's dictation of our diet ended. California and Florida and Texas moved into the corner grocery. The markets and manufacturers of the world moved into the village square. One need no longer plan on bequeathing his broadcloth suit or his wife's silk dress to the children. Goods, medicines, news, tools, hours of labor, hours of leisure — touch man's consciousness anywhere and you find it a more elastic, a freer consciousness. The cities grew but also the differentiation between city and country began to disappear. The theater moved into the village hall. Then the theater and the concert hall and the editorial page moved into the sitting room. The American's diet changed, his clothes changed, his health grew better and his life longer, fewer of his children were crippled. He no longer held his wife's property. His wife was not under legal compulsion to obey him. She might work in his office or serve on a jury. She had shed her petticoats and was shedding her political inferiority and, with it, immemorial social taboos.

In this new world man's consciousness was expanding and growing more complex. Also it was growing more tense. For if life was accelerating, it was also growing more precarious. Innumerable strains had been added. If the villages grew to towns and the towns to cities, old sanctions and constraints lost their force and many old securities were gone. The villager had lived among intimates whose solidarity gave him confidence; the burgher lived among strangers and, if with greater privacy, then also in greater anxiety. If the national culture had been diversified by the incorporation of many European cultures, that increase necessarily weakened the inheritance of the early republican culture. If the dictatorship of space was ended, so was the familiarity of place. If an always mobile people grew increasingly mobile, they paid for it in that mobility lessened the strength of familiar surroundings, ingrained habits, and the tranquillity of permanence. If classes were more fluid, the privileges and prerogatives and immunities of an order felt

to be stable were withdrawn. If electric lights, tele-
phones, automobiles, hard roads, express trains, cities, a
widened franchise, increased man's control of his environment, they also added burdens to his unconscious. An
invention, Chesterton once said, is an incurable disease.
At least it is an irreversible social action, and the expanding energies laid heavier weights of choice on the human
soul.

Moreover, these strains were abetted by others. The
sanctions and prohibitions of religion had been steadily
weakening. If fear and superstition lessened, so did still
another kind of security, another certainty which had
relieved the individual of the duty of choice. All freedoms have a price and the modern world has found that
its freedoms must be paid for with strains. Moreover, the
new strains were interdependent. If religion lost its sanction, the sanctions of family life and of citizenship and
of the countryside were bound up with one another —
and with the automobile — and the flow of goods — and
the course of education. The impaired authority of a
priest or a father or a congressman, a city dweller's im-
munity from prying neighbors, a town's treatment of
graft or its ideas of immorality, were all bound up with
what the automobile was doing to space, with what the
steel mills were forging in Pittsburgh, and with the doctrines preached by professors of philosophy at colleges
whose social and racial groupings had changed.

The individual had become freer and more powerful.
He had also become more bound and helpless. And there

had been added to his consciousness an onerous burden of choice, conflict, strain, and tension which tended to become unbearable. The individual's consciousness grew more complex but it could not keep pace with the increasing complexity of the world he lived in. The new energies that had been loosed in the world forced mankind, as Freud said, to live psychologically beyond its means. Characteristic modern feelings developed — feelings of internal conflict, the free-floating, enveloping anxiety that feeds on itself. It enhanced the tendency to regress to simpler, more elemental levels of consciousness, to escape into more primitive states of being. The mind of man grew slowly, the modern world grew desperately fast. The mind of man was adaptable but not adaptable enough to keep pace with the changes in its carapace.

In 1898 the United States went to war with Spain. Our venture in imperialism followed. The energies I have mentioned went on gathering momentum. The dislocations, economic, political, financial, social, grew more severe. Between 1900 and 1914 the American equilibrium moved into new phases. In 1914 the World War broke out at last and it was certain that we should be involved in it, as we had been in six earlier world wars. In 1917 we went to war. In 1918 we provided the weight that swung the scales out of balance. In 1919 we refused the responsibility in world reorganization which our power had thrust on us. In 1920 we ratified the refusal and — so some of us believe — made inevitable another world war, which we must fight in order to free our power toward world reorganization.

These, then, were some of the forces that had acted on the United States of 1920. Think of any literary appraisal of our culture, whether Herbert Croly's superficial sociological system, or Mr. Santayana's esthetic subtleties, or the more orthodox systems of the literary critics I have described. Bring them to bear on the changing culture and they are at once seen to be incompetent instruments, instruments so meager and so fragile that they could make no effective contact. They did not at all enable writers to describe American life, past or present. The spate and avalanche I have alluded to never came within their scope at all. They did not equip writers to describe American life but only to describe the emotions of writers.

For the nation which came out of the war into the 1920's was hardly in any particular what the appraisers said it was. Our critics found it drab, cheerless, anemic, without hope, a decadent society. It was the most cheerful and energetic society in the world and, whether in envy or admiration, foreigners marveled that so much youth and so much hope could be left anywhere. At the very moment when literary critics were turning from us disgusted with industrial materialism and invoking the Russians as the only people who had a hopeful vision for mankind, with the most sedulous and imitative care the Russians were doing their utmost to reproduce the industrial materialism of America, in which they thought they had found the only hopeful vision for mankind. At the moment when criticism was describing America as a deadly uniformity of thought, belief, ideal, behavior, and social pattern, America was the most variegated and diversified society that the world had ever seen. It was a welter of conflicting thought, beliefs, ideals, behavior, classes, interests, racial stocks, sectional sentiments, education, economies, social systems, philosophies, patterns, and cultures. It was a heterogeneity so vast, so diversely composed, and in such rapid flux that no formula could express it, no generalization could contain it, and no system of ideas could subject it to control. At the very moment when literature was describing the Americans as dull, brutish, and slaves, they were the freest, the most colorful, and the most reckless people in the world.

As the 1920's came on, then, much that had been familiar and traditional in American life was either dead or dying. Much that was new, strange, and revolutionary was already upon us; more was on the way. Old energies had been accelerated, new energies had been released. In racial stocks, social and economic classes, interests, beliefs, cultures, this was a changed and changing nation. Innumerable old patterns had been broken, innumerable new patterns were forming. The nation had the greatest mechanical power, the greatest actual wealth, and very likely the greatest potential wealth in the world. It had the longest experience at self-government, the most flexible political institutions, incomparably the most flexible social institutions that history had ever seen. It had the greatest measure of democracy, the greatest freedom, the greatest social kindliness, the greatest degree of social justice, the greatest hope.

Also it contained many offenses, injustices, inequities, cruelties, and many possibilities that these would grow worse. Within it were conflicts, dislocations which grew graver, counterrevolutions, internal warfare of systems, exploitations, wastes, corruption. Many of the new energies were working evil and threatened to work worse evil. Much that was fine had been lost; the loss of more was possible. The continuity that had been preserved through fourteen decades of change was menaced, might possibly be destroyed. To these possibilities were added stresses from without, as old orders collapsed in Europe and new orders struggled to establish themselves there and in Asia.

It was a bewildering future — and an inspiring one. The nation was confused. But it was not dismayed — nor frightened — nor craven — nor decadent.

We may adopt the highest literary ground and remark that here was a challenge to writers. Our society greatly needed laborious study, patient exploration, sympathetic understanding. Furthermore, if literature likes variety, color, vigor, richness, intensity, flow and movement, the jewelry of lights and shifting patterns, here was perhaps the greatest wealth ever offered to it. Again, if it is a function of literature to participate in the solution of common problems, to explain, to interpret — if, that is, literature has an organic place in culture — then

surely here was its greatest opportunity in the American
history.

We have seen the outcome. Study, patience, sympathy, and understanding were precisely the instruments
which literature refused to bring to its job. An organic
relationship with culture was precisely what literature
refused to establish. Instead of studying American life,
literature denounced it. Instead of working to understand American life, literature repudiated it. By voluntary act it withdrew from the very activity which it insisted was its proper business. Few will say that it accepted its responsibility or made use of its opportunity.
Mr. MacLeish, Mr. Brooks, and innumerable penitents
who have lately been tailoring sackcloth to their own
measure acknowledge the failure. I have been discussing
it as a betrayal, and yet the emphasis must not be on betrayal, for the generality of writers, as I pointed out,
were moved by the highest idealism. The emphasis must
be put on the inadequacy of means — on the ineffective-
ness of purely literary ideas to make literary expression
an organic part of culture.

It remains to speak briefly of the effect on literature
itself. During the Twenties and thereafter there were
confusion and decay of values, there was anarchy of
thought and feeling, in American life. But in our literature there were immensely greater confusion and decay
of values, and the comprehensive word for it between
wars is anarchy. The society was rugged, lively, and
vital, but literature became increasingly debilitated,

capricious, querulous, and irrelevant. Unquestionably many lives went down in despair but society never felt that it was futile, whereas literature came increasingly to confess its own futility. Even in the dreadful years of the early 1930's, when the most severe strains ever put on us made the nation face common failures new to the national consciousness, the generality of Americans felt no such despair as literature felt. It was writers, not the American people, who believed that the promise of American life had ended.

We must not permit ourselves the easy appeal to the last argument of kings. To escape into the rhetoric or the obscurantism of war emotions would be a species of literary trick. Yet it is invincibly true that danger brings clarification and that in this way war has an edge which cuts through unrealities. As the universal war drew nearer to the United States something fundamental, something eternally simple, became clear. The Americans have changed as their society has changed, but their vigor, their courage, and especially their faith had not changed in accordance with the literary repudiation. The nation had not doubted its strength, its greatness, or its future. And, oddly, literary people were suddenly saying so. It is with no idea of vindicating or disproving literary ideas that Americans have gone out to die in defense of our common ways of life, and in defense of the implicit faith that animates them — precisely as Americans had always done in the past which was held to be ignoble. It is not to reassure intellectuals that the nation has overturned the calculations of its enemies who knew that it was decadent, weak, and incapable of meeting the tests of the modern world. There was no such intention; the nation did not take the literary ideas into account and for the most part did not know that they existed. The point is that the literary ideas were wrong. The point is that the American people were not what their writers had believed them to be. The point is that only persons so lost in logic, dream, and theory that they were cut off from their heritage could have held those ideas.

Something final is said about the literature we have been discussing when we observe that it took a world war to reveal to writers truths about the culture they sprang from which had been the commonplace knowledge of every man of sense, the ordinary experience of everyone who lived in touch with the American realities. Come back to that remark of Edmund Wilson's which I have quoted and am impelled to contemplate with reverence unalloyed. Mr. Wilson said, in effect: Never before in any country or any age had writers so savagely and so continually attacked the culture which had produced them. He cannot be gainsaid but there is a complement. Never in any country or any age had writers so misrepresented their culture, never had they been so unanimously wrong. Never had writers been so completely separated from the experiences that alone give life and validity to literature. And therefore because separation from the sources of life makes despair, never had literature been so despairing, and because false writing makes trivial writing, never had literature been so trivial.

That, then, is where we come out. The characteristic literature of our age has not been serious, it has been a trivial literature. Despair is an automatic result of separation from the common life. Triviality is an automatic penalty imposed by that common life. In our time writers have been more widely read, more enthusiastically applauded, and rewarded with greater wealth and public honors than writers have ever had before. Nearly any writer could get an audience, nearly any writer could lead a coterie, nearly any writer could have the appurtenances of distinction, nearly any competent writer could be famous, and many writers became rich. In superficial public esteem, in publicity, in money, writers in our time have ranked higher than any writers before them anywhere. And yet there is no escape from a realization that, while bestowing all this on writers, the public has more than half-consciously degraded them to the status of entertainers. If a writer has not been equated with a movie actor or a baseball player, at least he has been understood to be a worker in the same field. If literature has been understood to differ from the crafts of illusionists, acrobats, and stripteasers, it has also been understood to be performing the same social function.

The public has been glad to reward its entertainers but has not supposed that literature was speaking for the American people. Fame writers might have, but authority they have been steadily denied. Mr. Mencken or

Mr. Lewis has not been granted the authority that was freely accorded to Mark Twain. Neither Mr. Hemingway nor Mr. Brooks nor Mr. Jeffers has been granted the jurisdiction over the American spirit freely exercised by Emerson with the consent of his readers. Neither Mark Twain nor Emerson supposed that the Americans were the children of light or that America was the Kingdom of Heaven come upon earth. Both spoke rebukes to their countrymen so fundamental that anything said by writers in our time seems, by comparison, weak, captious, ephemeral, and a trifle effeminate. But both spoke with authority to a people who acknowledged their authority — because both spoke knowing whereof they spoke, and both spoke from within.

In the long arc of time when history comes to describe the culture of America between the two wars, it will not be American ideas or the American way of life that looks tawdry, cheap, empty, and base. It will be the half-bushel of writers who presumed to find them so on the basis of a blend of arrogance, ignorance, and beautiful ideas which would seem craven except that it is first of all ridiculous. Seeking for a phrase which will convey the quality of that literature, history may sum it up as the Age of Ignominy. "We must begin by thinking of American literature," the topic sentence may read, "not as functional in American life but as idle, dilettante, flippant, and intellectually sterile." The age of literary folly. The age of slapstick.

It would be pleasant to end these lectures as from a

headland with the sea beyond. I should like to tell you that I hear the fiddles tuning all over America. I should like to promise you that a generation of writers of more seasoned intelligence, of greater wisdom, more serious, more deeply dedicated, are now laying the foundations on which at last will be erected a literature worthy of a great people. And in fact there is a haste of literary people to exalt democracy, to exult in the native grain, and even to inquire and examine and search out what these things may be. American literature is wearing jeans, eating grits and sidemeat, gathering at the crossroads store to take a stand on the preamble to the Declaration of Independence. The American writer has unbuttoned the collar of his flannel shirt, is grinding corn between two hand-smoothed stones, and has undertaken to re-create his personality with the proper proportions of Daniel Boone and Walt Whitman. His eyes have seen the glory of the coming of the Lord. O beautiful for spacious skies, for amber waves of grain, he sings with a loving and compassionate heart.

But I confess uneasiness. I am not yet an old man but already in my time I have seen this same eagerness and compassion expanded in many contradictory causes, this same literary personality dedicated to many disparate values with the same fervor. I cannot believe that ignorant love is more stable than ignorant contempt. The literary man loving freedom, who lately derided it as a superstition and a weakness of the plutocracies? The literary man praising the American way, who only a few hours back found in it nothing but absurdity? The literary man associating himself as with brothers of one heart with the democracy who yesterday were the boobs, the suckers, the fall guys, the Rotarians, the coarse-souled materialists of all the world? Well, maybe, but one long seasoned in folly may be permitted to add, probably not for long. The generality of writers of my time have suggested to me that the literary temperament is unstable and I must doubt if Almighty God has chosen the 1940's to make it over for all time. In some purple evening there will be another floodlighted opening at Grauman's Chinese Theater and worshipful thousands will discover that Miss Veronica Lake has let her hair down over her right eye. By noon the next day millions of girls will be looking at life with the left eye only and, the weary expectation is, resolute and one-eyed literary folk will once more be beholding the land of broken promises, inhabited only by inferior people who destroy individuality and break the Artist's heart.

Neither God nor nature has decreed ways in which books must be written. Literature is not subject to the laws which bring forth Mazzaroth in his season and guide Arcturus with his sons. It is subject to writers, mortal men all, men not notable for fixity of character, suffering much from neurosis, much given to whim, caprice, suggestibility, and mistaking the quirks of their emotions for the contours of objective fact. Books will continue to be written by writers. They will faithfully present the ideas and emotions of writers. When those ideas and emotions chance to be true or great, books will be true and great. When they chance to be childish or frivolous or silly, books will correspond. I cannot tell you what literature will be like when you have fought through the war and taken citizenship in the unpredictable world of the future. But, a literary man, I too can succumb to the persuasiveness of literary ideas — I can tell you a moral which the writers of my time have pointed for the writers of your time. I can tell you what literature will have to do if it is to be what, in the faraway, expectant dawn of my era, it set out to be.

If literature is to be a dependable description of America, if it is to make a useful comment on America, then first of all it must know America. The word "ignorance" has had to run through these lectures like a leitmotif. For the guesses, phantasies, and deductions which contented so many of the writers we have talked about, it must substitute patient years — years of study, years of experience. Knowledge is a slow growth, a long path beset with possibilities of error. Men are not given to know the nature of things by intuition. Authority is not born full-grown in any mind, nor can anyone come to it by staring into his own soul, or at his navel, or into the high priest's emerald breastplate. No one can know a country or a people, no one can know even the small portions with which most of us must be content, except by a long effort to know them, a refusal to be satisfied with the nobly vague, a distrust of the logically beautiful. Knowledge does not come from the matching up of myths, abstractions, and hypotheses that made the writers of the 1920's sure they were red to the shoulders with the blood of life when they were only watching the play of shadows across the screen of their own souls. Knowledge means sweat and doggedness, a realization that one can never know enough, and it comes from experience inappeasably sought after and tested with the most powerful reagents the mind can use. Writers must be content to hold their peace until they know what they are talking about. Readers must be willing to hold them to the job if they refuse to hold themselves. An uninstructed gentleness toward writers has been the mistake of readers in our time. Words like "fool" and "liar" might profitably come back to use. If literature is a trivial pursuit, folly and lying are of no particular moment, but if literature is to be serious then it cannot be permitted folly and lying and when they appear in it they must be labeled and denounced.

Yet knowledge can be come by. But first there is a fixed barrier which writers cannot cross except by virtue of a profound humility. The moral of our literature between the wars is that literature must come upon futility and despair unless it begins in fellowship from within. Rejection, the attitude of superiority, disdain of the experience of ordinary people, repudiation of the values to which the generality of a writer's countrymen devote their lives — the literature of my generation tried that path and found that the path ended in impotence and the courtship of death. The evils and abuses of society

may be intolerable but my generation has proved that
literature can do nothing whatever about them from outside. It must enter in, it must speak its "Thou shalt!" as
one who shares the dust and thirst. Cut the umbilical
cord and what dies is not society but literature. Form
coteries of the initiate, turn in abhorrence from the village square to the High Place, consecrate yourself to
anything which the louts at the foot of the High Place
cannot know, however fine or noble or beautiful it may
be — and in the end you have only a group of the merely
literary, speaking fretfully to one another in soft voices
while the tides of the world sweep by.

Either literature deals honestly with the basic experiences in which all men may see themselves, or else it is
only a mannered diversion practised by the impaired
and of interest only to the leisure moments of those who
are whole. Either it is a man and a brother speaking to
men and brothers, speaking of the things which all share
and are subject to, or else it is only a private titillation.
Well over a century ago Ralph Waldo Emerson ordered
the American writer to his job — to the meal in the firkin,
the milk in the pan. To know what it was that had appeared upon the earth, the new man, this American. To
search his heart, his mind, his vision, his memory. Only
in obeying that command has American literature ever
found reality. Our literature can be true only as it is
true of us, it can be great only as it comes to find greatness. All roots will be winterkilled and all the sweet
green shoots will die except as they are warmed and

fertilized by the common experience of Americans. That common experience is sufficiently wide and deep — literature has never yet drawn even with it and can never exhaust it. In it lies the future of American literature, possibly a great future, but only as the writers of the future, by their own wit or by the grace of God, may, as the writers between wars in the main did not, accept it as their own.

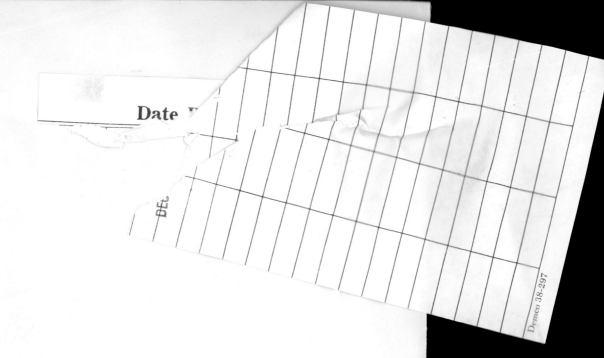

Date